Gillian Wearing, *Sixty Minute Silence*

余震：英国当代艺术展 1990-2006
Aftershock: Contemporary British Art 1990-2006

湖南美术出版社

主办单位:
Presented By:

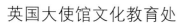
英国大使馆文化教育处

首都博物馆
CAPITAL MUSEUM CHINA

中央美術學院
Central Academy of Fine Arts

余震：英国当代艺术展 1990-2006
Aftershock: Contemporary British Art 1990-2006

英国大使馆文化教育处

湖南美术出版社

英国文化协会是一个提供学习机会和加强文化关系的国际性机构。

在中国，英国文化协会作为英国驻北京大使馆的文化教育处以及英国驻上海、广州和重庆总领事馆的文化教育处开展工作。

英国文化协会特别编写并出版此书，以配合在广东美术馆以及首都博物馆举办的展览"余震：英国当代艺术展1990－2006"。

广东美术馆：广州市二沙岛烟雨路38号
2006年12月15日－2007年2月4日

首都博物馆：北京西城区复兴门外大街16号
2007年3月20日－5月11日

策展人：
秦思源，策划部主任兼副馆长，尤伦斯当代艺术中心，北京
郭晓彦，广州三年展办公室负责人，广东美术馆策展人，广州
皮力，独立策展人，UniversalStudios-beijing 总监
理查德·赖利，展览中心主任，视觉艺术部，英国文化协会，伦敦

展览执行小组：
艾米莉·巴特尔，展人助理，视觉艺术部，英国文化协会，伦敦
赵　丽，艺术经理，英国大使馆文化教育处，北京
梁俊红，艺术官员，英国大使馆文化教育处，北京
曾咏江，艺术经理，英国总领事馆文化教育处，广州
刘晓华，艺术官员，英国总领事馆文化教育处，广州

The British Council is the United Kingdom's international organisation for cultural relations and self development opportunities.

In China we operate as the Cultural and Education Section of the British Embassy in Beijing, and the Cultural and Education Section of the British Consulates-General in Shanghai, Guangzhou and Chongqing.

Published on the occasion of the exhibition "Aftershock: Contemporary British Art 1990-2006" organised by the British Council in association with Guangdong Museum of Art, Guangzhou and Capital Museum, Beijing.

Guangdong Museum of Art, 38 Yanyu Road, Er-sha Island, Guangzhou
15 December 2006 – 4 February 2007

Capital Museum, 16 Fuxingmen Wai Street, Xicheng District, Beijing
20 March – 11 May 2007

Exhibition Curated by:
Colin Chinnery, Chief Curator and Deputy Director, Ullens Center for the Arts, Beijing
Guo Xiaoyan, Deputy Director of Guangzhou Triennial, Curator of Guangdong Museum of Art, Guangzhou
Pi Li, independent curator and Director of UniversalStudios-beijing
Richard Riley, Head of Exhibitions, Visual Arts, British Council, London

Exhibition Coordinated by:
Emily Butler, Assistant Curator, Visual Arts, British Council, London
Zhao Li, Arts Manager, Cultural and Education Section of the British Embassy, Beijing
Liang Junhong, Arts Officer, Cultural and Education Section of the British Embassy, Beijing
Florence Zeng, Arts Manager, Cultural and Education Section of the British Consulate-General, Guangzhou
Susan Liu, Arts Officer, Cultural and Education Section of the British Consulate-General, Guangzhou

Design and catalogue production by:
BAO-Chartered Room Investments Limited, Beijing

Edited by:
Emily Butler, Liang Junhong, Richard Riley

Cover photographs by Tony Law
Incorporating *Sixty Minute Silence*, 1996 by Gillian Wearing, © the artist, courtesy Maureen Paley, London

前言 / Foreword 2

英国文化协会 / British Council
广东美术馆 / Guangdong Museum of Art, Guangzhou
首都博物馆 / Capital Museum, Beijing

20世纪90年代英国文化简史/A Brief Cultural History in the 1990s 10

——迈克尔·布雷斯威尔 / Michael Bracewell

在震动之后 / After the Shock 24

——皮力 / Pi Li

艺术家及作品 / The Artists and Works 34

——艾米莉·巴特尔编写 / Texts by Emily Butler

杰克·查普曼和迪诺斯·查普曼 / Jake and Dinos Chapman 36

翠西·艾敏 / Tracey Emin 48

道格拉斯·戈登 / Douglas Gordon 58

莫娜·哈透姆 / Mona Hatoum 66

达明安·赫斯特 / Damien Hirst 76

加里·休姆 / Gary Hume 84

莎拉·卢卡斯 / Sarah Lucas 92

马克·奎安 / Marc Quinn 104

山姆·泰勒-伍德 / Sam Taylor-Wood 112

马克·渥林格 / Mark Wallinger 122

吉莉安·韦英 / Gillian Wearing 130

参展作品 / List of Works 140

英国文化协会 / British Council
沙利文 / Michael O'Sullivan
安德利亚 · 罗斯 / Andrea Rose

广东美术馆 / Guangdong Museum of Art, Guangzhou
王璜生 / Wang Huangsheng

首都博物馆 / Capital Museum, Beijing
郭小凌 / Guo Xiaoling

前言 / Foreword

英国文化协会十分高兴与广东美术馆和首都博物馆合作，在中国举办这一题为"余震：英国当代艺术展1990－2006"的新展览。

展览将为中国观众带来英国20世纪90年代早中期最为卓越也最具代表性的12位艺术家的主要作品。这个新生的艺术家群体，运用严密的智慧，创造者的领悟力，和他们都市化的幽默，曾给英国的艺术世界带来了一场猛烈的风暴，也重新确立了伦敦作为世界艺术之都之一的重要地位。当代艺术，因此也随着越来越多的展览的举办，成了媒体和大众讨论的一个热门话题。2000年春季伦敦第一个现当代艺术博物馆，现代泰特美术馆的创建，便是一个成功的例证。

"余震"这个名字意指这一近期的艺术馈赠，和它还在延续的影响。挑选出的这些艺术家的作品，虽然在过去的十年里经历了政治和社会的不断变化，却仍然保持着它们具有争议性的权威和震撼力，引发了公众对当代艺术的激烈争论。本次展览将展出艺术家们90年代的标志性作品和最新的创作。

展览作品由三位中国专业人士和两位英国文化协会视觉艺术部的同事挑选：郭晓彦，广东美术馆广州三年展办公室负责人；皮力，独立策展人，北京UniversalStudios-beijing总监；秦思源，前英国大使馆文化教育处艺术经埋，现任尤伦斯当代艺术中心副馆长兼策划部主任；理查德·赖利，英国文化协会伦敦视觉艺术部展览中心主任，以及他的助理艾米莉·巴特尔。我们对他们为展览的成功举办所作出的巨大贡献和努力表示由衷的感谢。

同时，也对英国文化协会驻中国办公室的同事：北京办公室的赵丽、梁俊红和广州办公室的曾咏江、刘晓华表示诚挚的谢意，感谢他们从一开始就为展览付出的艰辛努力。另外，也请允许我们对视觉艺术专题研究小组负责人加勒斯·休斯和为准备展览提供技术支持的团队表达感激之情，更要感谢中央美术学院对此次展览在中国的顺利举办给予我们的大力支持和协助。

我们也一如既往地，对接受了我们的邀请并热情参与展览的艺术家们，和他们的画廊以及代理人，表达最诚挚的谢意。对那些慷慨提供作品给我们展出的收藏家们表示我们最热切的谢意。感谢皮力以中国文化的立场和他对英国当代艺术的敏锐洞察力为画册撰写的文章，以及迈克尔·布雷斯威尔对英国近期文化史上这一非同寻常的时期所写的概览，也感谢艾米莉·巴特尔为画册精心编写的对参展艺术家们和他们的作品的介绍。

此外，我们对下面所有为这次展览的成功举办付出努力的朋友们，表示最诚挚的谢意：

洛拉·阿莱耶；马库斯·亚历山大；玛特·阿瑟斯；朱莉安·巴罗；霍诺尔·贝尔德；凯特·布莱克；艾琳·布拉德伯里；亚历克斯·布拉德利；莉齐·凯里-汤姆斯；苏珊娜·奇泽姆；路易斯·克拉克；托尼·康纳；吉尔·康斯坦丁；克里斯蒂·考廷；保利娜·达利；米歇尔·董；卡罗琳·道格斯；戴安娜·埃克尔斯；方茗；葆拉·费尔德曼；萨拉·吉勒特丹·冈恩；安德鲁·格威廉斯；汤姆·黑尔；约翰·哈金斯；卡琳·霍金；郝霖；汉娜·亨特；苏珊娜·海曼；晋华；李婧；林卓敏；林宁俭；娜丁·洛克；卢笙；萨拉·麦克唐纳；路易斯·梅钦；安娜·马里斯；露西·梅；苏珊·梅；科斯坦萨·马佐尼；安德里·莫斯特拉斯；玛丽安娜·马尔维；黄丽虹；牛兆麟；莫琳·佩利；潘月萍；蕾·佩特曼；裴南；安德利亚·施里克；邵珊；沈衍；尼克尔·西莫斯·达·席尔瓦；玛丽亚·斯塔伊；田霏雨；克拉里·沃里斯；王莉莉；吴茜平；倪韦伯；基特·韦尔斯；徐佳；姚安；俞菲

沙利文
英国文化协会中国地区主任
英国大使馆文化参赞

安德利亚·罗斯
英国文化协会
视觉艺术部总监

The British Council is delighted to be collaborating with Guangdong Museum of Art, Guangzhou and Capital Museum, Beijing in presenting "Aftershock: Contemporary British Art 1990-2006", a new exhibition created especially for China.

The exhibition provides audiences in China with the first opportunity to see major works by twelve of the most significant artists who came to prominence in Britain during the early-mid 1990s. With a combination of intellectual rigour, entrepreneurial savvy and street-wise humour, this new generation of artists took the art world by storm and helped to reinstate London as one of the world's art capitals. Contemporary art became a hotly debated topic in the media and audiences for exhibitions multiplied, exemplified best by the phenomenal success of Tate Modern, London's first museum of modern and contemporary art, which opened in the spring of 2000.

The title "Aftershock" refers to this recent legacy and its ongoing effect, as well as reflecting on the fact that a decade on, the work of the selected artists still retains the power and authority to contribute to contemporary debate. The exhibition includes both iconic works from the 1990s and more recent work that reveals the artists' current practice.

The exhibition has been selected and organised by three specialists based in China working closely with colleagues in the British Council's Visual Arts department: Guo Xiaoyan, Deputy Director of Guangzhou Triennial, Guangdong Museum of Art, Guangzhou; Pi Li, independent curator and Director, UniversalStudios-beijing; Colin Chinnery, formerly Arts Manager, Cultural and Education Section of the British Embassy and now Chief Curator and Deputy Director, Ullens Center for the Arts, Beijing; and Richard Riley, Head of Exhibitions, assisted by Emily Butler, in Visual Arts, London. We are grateful to them all for their hard work and diligence in bringing the exhibition to fruition.

Thanks also go to the many British Council colleagues in China who have been closely involved with the exhibition from the outset. In particular we should like to express our thanks to Zhao Li and Liang Junhong in Beijing, and Florence Zeng and Susan Liu in Guangzhou. We would also like to acknowledge the support of Gareth Hughes, Visual Arts Workshop Manager, and the technical team involved in the preparation of the works for exhibition. In addition we wish to express our gratitude to the Central Academy of Fine Arts, Beijing for helping with the arrangements in bringing this exhibition to China.

We are, as ever, enormously indebted to the artists themselves, and to their galleries and agents, who have responded with enthusiasm to our invitation to take part in the exhibition. We should like to thank most warmly the lenders to the exhibition, whose generosity in parting with their works is greatly appreciated. Our thanks also go to the authors of the catalogue: to Pi Li for his insight into contemporary British art from a Chinese perspective, to Michael Bracewell for his overview of this fascinating period in recent British cultural history, and to Emily Butler for compiling the detailed catalogue entries.

To all of them and to those listed below we offer our warmest thanks:

Lola Aleje; Marcus Alexander; Matt Arthurs; Julian Barrow; Honor Beddard; Kate Blake; Irene Bradbury; Alex Bradley; Lizzie Carey-Thomas; Susannah Chisholm; Louise Clarke; Tony Connor; Jill Constantine; Christie Coutin; Pauline Daley; Michelle Dong; Caroline Douglas; Diana Eccles; Fang Ming; Paula Feldman; Sarah Gillett; Dan Gunn; Andrew Gwilliams; Tom Hale; John Harkins; Karine Hocking; Jim Hollington; Hannah Hunt; Susannah Hyman; Jin Hua; Li Jing; Angel Lin; Jake Lin; Nadine Lockyer; Jessy Lu; Sara Macdonald; Louise Machin; Anna Marris; Lucy May; Susan May; Costanza Mazzoni; Andry Moustras; Marianne Mulvey; Josephine Ng; Niu Zhaolin; Maureen Paley; April Pan; Pei Nan; Roy Pateman; Andrea Schlieker; Shao Shan; Jason Shen; Nicole Simoes da Silva; Maria Stahi; Philip Tinari; Clarrie Wallis; Veronica Wang; Neil Webb; Kit Wells; Cynthia Wu; Xu Jia; Yao An; Yu Fei

Michael O'Sullivan
Regional Director China, British Council
Counsellor (Cultural), British Embassy Beijing

Andrea Rose
Director of Visual Arts
British Council

前言 / Foreword

　　"余震：英国当代艺术展 1990 2006"是英国文化协会在广州和北京两地举办的一个专门面向中国观众，展示英国当代艺术的展览。展览将着重向中国观众展现英国当代艺术的重要阶段——"艺术爆炸"时期成长起来的12位声名显赫的艺术家的主要作品，这些作品有可能为中国观众提供一种全新的视觉体验。

　　"余震"也提示出英国当代艺术发展重要时期的艺术创作状态及其后续效应，同时反映了这样一个事实，即十年之后，尽管政治和社会发生诸多变化，但被挑选出的这些艺术家的作品仍然保留着其具有争议性的权威和力量。

　　广东美术馆将以开放的心态介绍英国当代艺术，希望这个展览以宽泛而概括的方式展现出英国当代艺术家总体的精神特质，以及他们对社会包括政治、种族、文化、生活、人性等等的态度和感知、表达方式，同时也希望展现出他们每个人独特的思维角度和气质；还有，对促进英国当代艺术发展的文化环境和艺术制度有所了解也是我们举办这次展览的初衷之一。所以，"余震"也将使用介绍和讨论的方式，引导观众思考当代英国艺术的一些成功经验，以及这一文化转型为国际艺术舞台带来的意义深远的影响。

　　感谢英国文化协会，和英国文化协会驻伦敦的理查德·赖利先生和艾米莉·巴特尔女士，英国驻广州总领事馆文化教育处的郝霖先生对展览得以在中国举办所作出的努力。

　　对所有参与这一展览的机构和个人，在此谨表热切的谢意。

　　更应该感谢所有的参展艺术家。

王璜生
广东美术馆馆长

"Aftershock: Contemporary British Art 1990-2006" was organised by the British Council specifically for Chinese audiences and will be exhibited in Beijing and Guangzhou. "Aftershock" represents an important phase in British contemporary art and will feature major works by twelve famous artists who came of age during the period of this 'artistic explosion.' These works may present Chinese audiences with a whole new visual experience.

In addition to showing the state of artistic creation during this important phase in British contemporary art history, the exhibition also presents the 'aftershocks' of this period. While the works may have been made in response to a particular period, despite the many political and social changes that have occurred in the past decade, the selected pieces still hold controversial authority and force.

The Guangdong Museum of Art presents British contemporary art with an open mind. We hope this exhibition will provide an overall view of the unique spirit of contemporary British artists and their attitudes, perceptions, and ways of expression regarding politics, religion, culture, life, human nature, and more. We also hope the exhibition will reveal the artists' individual perspectives and temperaments. Another motive for organising this exhibition is to promote understanding of the cultural environment of British contemporary artistic development and its art system. "Aftershock" provides an opportunity for discussion around art to guide the public toward thinking about some of the successes of contemporary British art as well as the influence this cultural transformation has for the international art world.

I would like to thank the British Council, Mr Richard Riley and Ms Emily Butler in London, and Mr Jim Hollington, Director of the Culture and Education Section of the British Consulate-General in Guangzhou for all their efforts in putting together this exhibition.

I would also like to extend my deep and sincere gratitude to all the organisations and individuals involved in the making of this exhibition.

Finally, I wish to thank all the artists.

Wang Huangsheng
Director, Guangdong Museum of Art

前言 / Foreword

　　自现代艺术肇始至今已逾百年，在这百余年的历史中，众多流派打破了欧洲传统写实主义绘画一统天下的局面，为世界艺术构建了一个多元的舞台。它们强调艺术个性，尊重个人创造的理念，强化了知识创作领域的人文意识，并将这种意识和理念由造型艺术领域渗透到社会的各个层面。

　　与传统写实主义艺术不同，19世纪末，现代艺术的艺术家们不满学院派缺乏表现力，只注重发展技艺手法的创作方法，提出创立"绘画艺术自身的独立价值"，"摆脱对文学、历史的依赖"，倡导"为艺术而艺术"的创作道路。一批批先锋艺术家回归原始，从原始艺术、希腊艺术、中世纪艺术以及各国民族艺术中汲取营养，积极探索造型艺术的形式语言，以求恢复艺术的活力。

　　首都博物馆与英国大使馆文化教育处共同举办的题为"余震"的英国当代艺术展，为观众呈现了12位英国当代艺术家的杰出作品。他们的作品用时尚、先锋的语言，阐释着他们在哲学层面上对社会和时代的思考。过去，我们对当代艺术了解较少，希望通过对这些作品的解读，更深层地认识当代艺术创作对一个时代的意义。

郭小凌
首都博物馆馆长

Modern art has existed for over a hundred years. During this period, many schools of art have broken down the all-encompassing universalism of traditional European realist painting, forging a pluralistic stage for artists all over the world. This new stage emphasizes the individualism of art, respects individual creativity, reinforces the humanitarian aspect of knowledge production, and disseminates these ideas and meanings from the realm of fine art to all levels of society.

By the end of the nineteenth century, contemporary artists were dissatisfied with the academic styles' lack of expressive power that only emphasised developing skills for production. They put forward the 'independent value of a painter', casting off their reliance on literature and history, and proposed 'art for art's sake' as a creative path. Avant-garde artists looked to their roots for inspiration, deriving nutrients from primitive art, classical Greek art, medieval art, and the ethnic art of different countries. They actively explored the formal language of fine art in order to resuscitate art's vitality.

Capital Museum and the British Council have jointly organised "Aftershock", an exhibition of contemporary British art featuring outstanding works by twelve living artists. Their works use a fresh new language to explain their philosophical views about society and current times. In the past, our understanding of contemporary art has been wanting. Hopefully through a deeper understanding of these works, we can gain a greater sense of the significance that contemporary art has for current times.

Guo Xiaoling
Director, Capital Museum

20世纪90年代英国文化简史 / A Brief Cultural History of Britain in the 1990s

迈克尔·布雷斯威尔
Michael Bracewell

不论以何种方式去估量，在20世纪80年代末到21世纪初，英国的社会和文化都充满了意义重大的转变，其中包括几乎动摇了英国现代社会根本基础的两件大事：一是执政将近20年的保守党在1997年轰然倒台，一是威尔士王妃戴安娜在同年死于非命。关于这些大事件的报道也反映出英国大众传媒高密度增长和不断变化的特点、媒体对公众意见的控制，以及政府和皇室的权力。

而90年代也同样是值得纪念的十年，因为当时无论是流行音乐、时尚、美术、媒体还是设计，都获得了一种全新的风格和态度，而且更为重要的是，这是对其文化状态的一次重新审视和部分融合。至于英国视觉艺术的再次繁荣，则是由被称为"英国青年艺术"的这一时代现象所促进的结果，我们也许可以将达明安·赫斯特1988年在伦敦策划的具有巨大影响力的群体展"冰冻"[Freeze]视为这一时期的开端，而将2000年5月现代泰特美术馆的开放视为其在公众艺术机构领域的一个纪念碑。

在90年代的英国，当代艺术在很多方面都成为城市复兴的首要动因。正因为如此，伦敦本身被赋予了新的活力，其时尚中心也从伦敦的西区转移到了靠近传统金融区的东区，很多年轻艺术家选择在那里居住和创作。同时，这个全新的艺术景象也同样促成了具有猛烈和愤世风格的"颓废"派思潮的复兴，该思潮第一次出现是在一个世纪以前，即19世纪末。

政治变动总是与文化变化相辅相成。首相玛格丽特·撒切尔所领导的保守党政府从1979年开始执政，直至1988年。期间很多进步人士和左翼文化人物都持有一个已深入人心的观点，那就是保守党政府的政策和思想并不怎么对艺术有好感，并且对于前卫文化持狭隘态度，甚至可以说对现代社会的很多东西都是轻视的。因此，贯穿差不多整个80年代，英国的视觉艺术是由一小撮伦敦西区的老派艺术赞助人所代表的，他们因为权威和财富被看做是老一辈中值得尊敬的一代。

1990年，玛格丽特·撒切尔被同为保守党的约翰·梅杰取代，由他继续领导着保守党政府执政，直至以托尼·布莱尔为代表的"新工党"在1997年选举中大获全胜。这种政治变动带来了一股代表着青春和变化的新风尚，由新一代的年轻艺术家、画廊专业人士和文化进步人士所代表。从很多方面来讲，托尼·布莱尔所领导的新工党最初对所有这些文化现象都表现出了极大兴趣并积极给予支持，这受到了民众的普遍欢迎，相比之下，之前的政府所采取的态度却是厌恶和极力摧毁，而且从某种程度上来说，新工党也试着在寻找可以和自身结成同盟的所谓文化复兴运动——是由年青一代在整个艺术领域所倡导的。

By any measure of estimation, British society and culture between the end of the 1980s and the opening years of the twenty-first century were filled with significant change. This would include two events which seemed to shake the very foundations of modern British society: the spectacular downfall, after nearly twenty years in power, of the Conservative government in 1997; and the violent death, during the same year, of Diana, Princess of Wales. The reporting of these events also revealed the increasing density and changing nature of Britain's mass media, and the hold of that media on public opinion and the power of government and royalty.

But the 1990s would also be remembered as a decade when pop music, fashion, fine art, media and design would all acquire new styles, new attitudes and, most important, a reassessment and partial conflation of their cultural status. As regards the renewed fashionability of the visual arts in Britain, prompted by the generational phenomenon known as 'Young British Art', this was a period which might be seen as beginning with the hugely influential group exhibition "Freeze", curated by Damien Hirst in London in 1988, and finding its institutional monument in the opening of Tate Modern in May, 2000.

In many ways, contemporary art would become the principal agent of urban regeneration in Britain in the 1990s. As a consequence of this, London itself would be regarded as newly vibrant - with the centre of fashionability moving from the West End of London to the East End, near the traditional financial and banking district, where many of the young artists chose to live and work. At the same time, there was the sense that this same new art scene was proposing a heady, cynical reinvention of the fin de siècle 'Decadence' which had first occurred a century earlier, in the closing decade of the nineteenth century.

Political change thus coincided with cultural change. In 1988, Prime Minister Margaret Thatcher's Conservative government had been in power since 1979. Amongst many more progressive or leftist cultural figures, there was the deeply held belief that the Conservative government's policies and ideology were unsympathetic towards the arts, intolerant of the avant-garde and even disdainful of large swathes of modern society. Throughout much of the 1980s, the visual arts in Britain were represented by a small group of old established art dealers in the West End of London, whose authority and wealth was seen to be that of an older, somewhat patriarchal generation.

In 1990, Margaret Thatcher would be replaced by her own party, and John Major's subsequent Conservative government would remain in power until Tony Blair's landslide victory as 'New Labour' in the election of 1997. This would introduce a new vogue for youthfulness and change, that would be mirrored by the new generation of young artists, gallerists and cultural entrepreneurs. In many ways, Tony Blair's New Labour would initially be welcomed as an active and interested supporter of all those cultural phenomena that the previous government had been seen to both resent and actively dismantle. And, to some extent, New Labour would seek to ally itself to what was regarded as a cultural renaissance, created across the arts by a new generation.

在80年代后半叶，一种最具争议性也最具知名度的新艺术开始在苏格兰崭露头角。被泛泛冠以"格拉斯哥新形象派"头衔的画家，如史蒂文·坎贝尔和艾德里安·威司涅夫斯基，所创作出的作品具有很深的文学性和新浪漫主义的气息，同时也是对欧洲绘画近期运动和发展的呼应。他们的作品积极运用了广为人知和富有争议的后现代主义风格，该流派提出了关于原创性、影响力、目的、讽刺和背景等艺术领域的问题。对于"格拉斯哥新形象派"的这些画家们来说，后现代主义被视为对焦虑、醒悟和浪漫主义极度失望的一个提示。

1988年，这种关注的趋势被新一代的年轻成员们所逆转过来。这些年轻人大多毕业于伦敦哥德史密斯学院，而且很多人彼此之间都有私交，他们被称作"英国青年艺术家"。那时，英国的艺术中心从格拉斯哥转移到了伦敦东区，英国当代艺术的风格也开始有所改变，通过广泛采用不同的媒介、材料和艺术创作过程，变得乐观向上、主张对抗、自我促进并且充满活力。影响 "英国青年艺术"的两大主要因素首先是曾在哥德史密斯学院授过课的英国艺术家迈克尔·克雷格·马丁，然后是一位前身是证券经纪人的美国艺术家杰夫·昆斯的作品。

"英国青年艺术家"，简称YBAs，在英国成为新文化意识的象征。他们富有争议的作品、几乎一夜成名的效应以及他们与媒体和时尚之间的关系，使他们像新工党一样，逐渐代表着一种新秩序——这被直接认为是社会和文化变革的动因。

随着"英国青年艺术"和"新工党"这两个名词的频繁使用，可以看出90年代英国社会和文化的基本特性，因为这个时期英国文化推崇的是年轻和国家认同感——这两种特性被认为具有相同的含义，体现了文化复兴的蓬勃活力。至此，前缀"Brit"被时髦地用作对British的缩写，很快就在全文化范围内被广泛采用，用来形容青春、新奇、时尚和实用性。

从很多方面来讲，90年代"英国文化"的构成与60年代中期大众文化和媒体的构成是极为相似的。比如对"英式风格"象征的迷恋、对所有老套东西的蔑视、对新技术的喜悦以及对性别特征和都市文化的欢声雀跃，这些都是60年代和90年代时尚所共享的关键因素。

这两个年代的相似之处通过两个主要因素得到证实并被表现出来。首先是英国国旗所代表的流行文化的复兴，此时英国国旗并非仅仅是一个代表英式风格的鲜明符号，更是一种时尚的声明和现代酷文化的标志。获得巨大成功的摇滚乐队 "绿洲"的吉他手——诺埃尔·加拉格尔在他演奏的吉他上装饰着英国国旗的图样。同样地，著名的"辣妹"组合成员姬芮·哈利维尔，也曾穿着英国国旗图样的迷你裙拍照。(i)

During the latter half of the 1980s, the most discussed and acclaimed new art had been emerging from Scotland. Painters such as Steven Campbell and Adrian Wiszniewski, grouped loosely under the label, 'New Image Glasgow', had made work which was deeply literary, neo-romantic and responsive to recent movements in European painting. Their work was also engaging with what had become known and increasingly discussed as the postmodern condition. This raised questions in art about authorship, influence, intention, irony and context. For the 'New Image Glasgow' painters, postmodernism was seen more as a prompt for anxiety, disillusion and romantic despair.

In 1988, the temper of these concerns was reversed by the young members of a new generation, many of whom were graduates of Goldsmiths College, London, most of whom knew one another personally, and who were labelled 'Young British Artists'. The artistic centre of Britain moved from Glasgow to East London, and the temperament of contemporary British art was changed, becoming upbeat, confrontational, self promotional and exuberant in its adoption of a wide range of media, materials and art-making processes. Two of the principal influences on 'Young British Art' would be the British artist Michael Craig Martin - then a tutor at Goldsmiths college - and the work of the American bond dealer turned artist, Jeff Koons.

The 'Young British Artists' would become emblematic of a new cultural sensibility within the UK. In their often controversial work and their almost immediate celebrity, as much as their relationship to media and "fashionability, the 'YBAs', like New Labour", came to represent a new order - directly regarded as agents of social and cultural change.

In the popularly used titles of these two phenomena - 'Young British Art' and 'New Labour' - one could identify two of the fundamental characteristics of British society and culture in the 1990s. For this was a period during which British culture made a fetish of both youth and national identity - the two qualities becoming seen as synonymous with one another, denoting a flamboyant spirit of cultural renewal. To this end, the prefix 'Brit' (as a funky abbreviation of 'British') was soon being used pan-culturally to describe youth, newness, fashionability and relevance.

In many ways, the constitution of 'BritCulture' during the 1990s would be very similar to that found in the popular culture and media of the middle years of the 1960s. An obsession with emblems of 'Britishness', a cult of disregard for all that was considered old, a delight in new technologies and a vivacious celebration of sexuality and urban culture were all key factors that were shared by the fashions of the 1960s and the 1990s.

The similarity between the two decades was both proven and celebrated by two main factors. Firstly, the rehabilitation by popular culture of the Union Jack as not just a vibrant symbol of Britishness, but as a fashion statement and an emblem of cool modernity. Noel Gallagher, the guitarist with the hugely successful rock band, Oasis, would play a guitar which had the Union Jack emblazoned on its body. (Likewise Geri Halliwell, of the equally successful pop group, Spice Girls, would be photographed wearing a mini dress made out of fabric printed with the Union Jack.) (i)

i

"辣妹"组合成员姬芮·哈利维尔在伦敦
英国音乐奖的现场表演
1997年2月
摄影：Richard Young/Rex Features

Geri Halliwell of the Spice Girls performing at the Brit Awards, London
February 1997
Photograph: Richard Young/Rex Features

从70年代晚期到差不多整个80年代，英国国旗被认为是流行文化里传统爱国主义的一个符号，或者，更为过火的说法是，它是极端民族主义的象征。例如，著名的流行歌手莫里西因为在歌里流露出深厚的情感并巧妙地运用了文化意象，曾被拥戴为新文化的英雄。可是，当他1992年在伦敦芬士贝利公园的露天演唱会上，将英国国旗系在腰间登台演出时，则被一些学者谴责为带有种族主义色彩。

然而到了90年代中期，英国国旗在流行文化里摆脱了其政治模糊性，而且作为无所不在的年轻活力标志，恢复了其在60年代的时尚里所扮演的角色。无论是诺埃尔·加拉格尔的吉他，还是姬芮·哈利维尔的衣服，都因此被认为是对现代英式风格的声明：直接传承了1965年著名流行乐队"谁人"的贝司手约翰·恩特威斯尔所穿的英国国旗外套(ii)，或是1965年由迈克尔·英格里什为坐落在卡尔纳比街（英国著名的时尚设计区）的Gear精品店设计的米字旗太阳镜。

另一个·似乎把90年代和60年代的社会思潮联系在一起的历史因素，即是对伦敦作为新兴"活动"中心的重新定位。在这种新形势下，文化复兴创造出一批新崛起的名人。1966年4月15日发行的美国《时代》杂志封面直接提到了这一现象，上面写着："伦敦！一个多姿多彩的城市"。这篇文章里最著名的一段宣言是："在这个由青年人所引领的十年里，伦敦又突然绽放了。她多姿多彩，呈现出一种新气象。"

如果说60年代的伦敦涌现了一批新的精英，比如年轻的电影明星（特雷斯·斯坦普，迈克尔·凯恩）、摄影师、模特（大卫·贝利、让·辛普顿）和流行音乐明星（"甲壳虫"乐队、"谁人"乐队、"庭鸟"乐队），那么90年代的伦敦可以说又重新获得了复兴。另一本美国杂志《名利场》曾经在1997年4月发行的期刊上强调过这一点，标题上写着："伦敦多姿多彩！再现辉煌(iii)。封面是利亚姆·加拉格尔（诺埃尔·加拉格尔的兄弟，同样是"绿洲"乐队的成员）的照片，他和他当时的女友即演员帕特西·肯西特一起躺在一张英国国旗床单上。

受一位当时在美国杂志《名利场》工作的英国记者托比·杨的想法影响，《时代》杂志早在30年前发表的言论再度流行起来，被许多别的杂志和报纸大肆征抄引用。"多姿多彩伦敦"的新阵营当然包括流行音乐明星、酒店企业人士、时尚设计师、电视工作者和模特，但如果要说其中最为显著的，那就不得不提到"英国青年艺术家"。

ii

"My Generation"专辑封面，"谁人"乐队的贝司手约翰·恩特威斯尔，身穿印有英国国旗的外套
1965

John Entwistle of The Who wearing a Union Jack jacket on the cover of the album "My Generation"
1965

Throughout the late 1970s and much of the 1980s, the Union Jack had been regarded within popular culture as either a symbol of traditional patriotism, or, more sinisterly, as the emblem of extreme nationalism. Indeed, the pop singer Morrissey - who had previously been hailed as a new cultural hero for his deeply emotive and cleverly poised use of cultural imagery in his songs - was accused of racism by some pundits when he wore a Union Jack flag tied around his waist during an open air concert in Finsbury Park, London, in 1992.

By the middle of the 1990s, however, the image of the Union Jack had been divested, pop culturally, of its political ambiguity. Rather, it had been restored to the role it once occupied in the fashions of the 1960s, as an ubiquitous signifier of youthful exuberance. Noel Gallagher's guitar or Geri Halliwell's dress would thus be regarded as statements of modern Britishness: direct descendants of the Union Jack jacket worn by John Entwistle of the pop group The Who, in 1965 (ii), or the Union Jack sunglasses designed by Michael English for the 'Gear' boutique on Carnaby Street, London, in 1965.

The other historical factor which seemed to relate the ethos of the 1990s to that of the 1960s was the re-positioning of London as the heart of a new 'scene', in which a cultural renaissance had created a new cast of celebrities. The immediate reference point was the cover of the American magazine, Time, for the issue dated April 15th, 1966: 'London: The Swinging City'. Famously, this article would pronounce: "In a decade dominated by youth, London has burst into bloom. It swings; it is the scene."

If London in the 1960s had seen a new elite of young film stars (Terence Stamp and Michael Caine, for example), photographers and models (David Bailey and Jean Shrimpton) and pop stars (The Beatles, The Who, The Yardbirds), then London in the 1990s would be claimed to have recaptured that spirit. The point was underlined by another American magazine, *Vanity Fair*, in its issue for April, 1997, with the headline, "London Swings Again!" (iii). The cover featured a photograph of Liam Gallagher (brother of Noel Gallagher, and also in the rock group Oasis) lying under a Union Jack bedspread with his then girlfriend, the actor Patsy Kensit.

From an idea originated by the British journalist, Toby Young, who was at that point working briefly in New York for *Vanity Fair*, this revival of the claims made by *Time* magazine three decades earlier would be ravenously seized upon by other magazines and newspapers. The cast of the new 'Swinging London' would include of course pop stars, restauranteurs, fashion designers, television presenters and models, but it would probably feature 'Young British Artists' most prominently of all.

iii

《名利场》
伦敦多姿多彩！再现辉煌
1997年3月
封面：利亚姆·加拉格尔和帕齐·肯西特

Vanity Fair
London Swings Again!
March 1997
Cover featuring Liam Gallagher and Patsy Kensit

实际上，提姆·诺柏和休·韦伯斯这两位艺术家曾借用《名利场》杂志的封面创作过一个作品——很简单，只是把艺术家的头部照片放到本来是加拉格尔和肯西特的封面上。（iv）同样地，早在1996年，位于美国明尼阿波利斯市的沃克艺术中心举办了一个展览，名为"精彩！来自伦敦的新艺术"['Brilliant!'New Art From London]，这与它在1965年举办的展览"伦敦：新景象"[London: The New Scene] 相比，只不过是一个直接的翻新。（尤其典型的是英国青年艺术家的定位和他们想要震撼观众的那种意图，如"精彩"展的画册封面展示了伦敦市近期受到恐怖分子炸弹袭击的街区。）(v)

90年代英国文化的首要特性包括一种对具有嘲讽性或有违常规的意象的喜悦、一种社会现实主义倾向以及一种热衷于反理性主义的做作。这样，英国文化就穿上讽刺的外衣，重新贴上都市生存能力的标签，转换为艺术创作的深奥语言，从而与小报新闻业和广告业共享价值。

可是尽管英国文化具有时尚性，但奇怪的是它却带有一种复古趋势。在朋克被视为是现代性本身的文化表达达到了临界物质状态时，其审美也成为了一种疯狂的未来主义。而90年代的英国文化在日常情形和陈规中似乎更为自在，让人依稀对70年代有些颓废的英国产生怀旧之情，同时它也是喜欢吸纳百川的文化，常常循环再现早些时期的流行文化风格。

"英国青年艺术"同样也拿自己的身份和言辞做文章，常常把粗俗的意象和愚钝的感情与高度自若和微妙的概念主义混杂在一起。很多英国青年艺术家在其早期生涯中所创作的作品就像是为吸引眼球而做的广告和生猛的笑话，戏剧、性和死亡由此成为"英国青年艺术"的意象和主题的首选。

作为后现代主义消费者的第一代，英国青年艺术家们提前掌握了先进的图像制作物理知识，在孩提时代就受到流行音乐、广告和电视的熏陶，并作为艺术学生学习了批判性理论，因此他们如此娴熟地在自己的作品里同时创造出具有喜剧性、模糊性以及高度操纵性的精神言论，也就不足为奇。从某种程度上来说，这是年轻艺术家们反对基于政治的文化论的一个群体反应，当时这种文化论在艺术学校占据着统治地位。因此，尽可能地表现粗俗和自私自利就成了这种新的审美风格至关重要的一部分。

因为持有这样的想法，年轻的艺术家山姆·泰勒-伍德才会拍摄她将裤子褪到脚踝的照片，并且戴着深色墨镜，穿着一件写着"性交、口交、虐待、手淫"字样的T恤衫；查普曼兄弟才利用儿童人体模型做原型创作了一系列作品，并通过为这些模型加上不恰当的男女生殖器而使其形象变得怪诞；而达明安·赫斯特则拍摄自己在太平间举着一个从死尸上分离下来的人头，像顽童一般咧着嘴笑。最为贴切的，也许是莎拉·卢卡斯，早期她在伦敦南部的竞赛城艺术项目空间举办的展览，是利用英国小报那些无道德的耸人听闻的标题来做成拼贴品。

iv

提姆·诺柏和休·韦斯伯
伦敦多姿多彩
1997
海报集成照片
70cm×48cm

Tim Noble & Sue Webster
London Swings
1997
Photomontage on Poster
70cm×48cm

The artists Tim Noble and Sue Webster, in fact, would make a work which parodied the *Vanity Fair* cover - simply placing photographs of the artists' heads over those of Gallagher and Kensit (iv). Likewise, as early as 1996, the Walker Art Center in Minneapolis, USA, had held its exhibition, " 'Brilliant!' New Art From London" as a direct update of its exhibition "London: The New Scene", held in 1965. (It was typical in the positioning of the 'Young British Artists', and the intention to shock viewers, that the cover of the catalogue for " 'Brilliant!' " depicted the streets in the City of London that had recently been devastated by a terrorist's bomb.) (v)

The principal characteristics of 'BritCulture' in the 90s would include a delight in irreverent or transgressive imagery, a propensity for social realism and an affectation of devout anti-intellectualism. In this it would share the values of tabloid journalism and advertising, transposed to the sophisticated language of fine artistic production, coated in a thick layer of irony and re-labelled as streetwise.

But despite its fashionability, the temper of 'BritCulture' was curiously archaic. Where punk had seemed liked the cultural expression of modernity itself reaching critical mass, its aesthetic achieving a kind of crazed futurism, the 'BritCulture' of the 1990s seemed more at ease with the quotidian and the banal, nostalgic for some damp, half remembered Britain of the 1970s. It was also a culture that was steeped in quotation, often recycling pop cultural styles from earlier periods.

'Young British Art' would also play games with its own identity and rhetoric, often mixing lumpen imagery and crass sentiments with highly poised and nuanced conceptualism. During their early careers, many of the 'YBAs' made work which resembled both eye-grabbing advertising campaigns and crude jokes. Comedy, sex and death were therefore uppermost in the imagery and themes of 'Young British Art'.

As the first generation of postmodern consumers, precociously advanced in the physics of image-making, raised as children on pop music, advertising and television, and as art students on critical theory, it was perhaps hardly surprising that the 'YBAs' proved so skilful in making simultaneously comedic, ambiguous, and deeply manipulative moral statements within their work. In some ways, this was a generational reaction by young artists against the politically based cultural theory which had previously held sway in the art schools. Thus, to appear as crass and self-serving as possible became a vital part of the new aesthetic.

With this in mind, the young Sam Taylor-Wood would photograph herself with her trousers pulled down to her ankles, wearing dark glasses and a T-shirt which had the words, 'Fuck, Suck, Spank, Wank' printed on it in bold letters; Jake and Dinos Chapman would make mannequins of children, whose features were then grotesquely disfigured by attached models of male and female genitalia; Damien Hirst would be photographed in a morgue, impishly grinning as he held up a severed human head. Most pertinently, perhaps, Sarah Lucas would have an early exhibition at the City Racing art project space in South London, of work based on collages of tabloid newspapers, blaring their lurid headlines of debased moral hysteria.

v

"'精彩!'来自伦敦的新艺术"
沃克艺术中心，美国明尼阿波利斯，
1995年10月22日到1996年1月7日；
休斯敦当代艺术馆，
1996年2月17日至4月14日
画册封面

"'Brilliant!' New Art from London"
Walker Art Center, Minneapolis
October 22 1995- January 7 1996 and
Contemporary Arts Museum, Houston
February 17 – April 14 1996
Catalogue Cover

英国青年艺术家们这些早期的作品很有效地吸引了公众的注意，并引起了很大争议，而且得到贵族阶级的权力经纪，对他们来说，艺术大众文化的这些作品和其创作过程都简直是太匪夷所思了。因此，广告业界的显赫人物查尔斯·萨奇成为第一个真正对这些艺术家的作品感兴趣的收藏家也就顺理成章，在80年代甚至于保守党都是他的客户。1997年萨奇在伦敦皇家艺术学院举办了一个收藏展，名为"感觉：萨奇收藏的英国青年艺术家作品"(vi)，每天都吸引了三千名左右的参观者。这个展览以展品的呈现方式而瞩目：作品大多聚焦于暴力的死亡题材。

从很多方面来说，90年代的主要文化主题似乎都聚焦在威尔士王妃戴安娜这个悲剧人物身上，她于1997年8月在巴黎死于一场意外车祸而让世人震惊。在"感觉"展上，甚至有记者提出建议，认为应该将展厅中心那幅具有争议性的儿童杀手梅若·亨德利的肖像摘下，用戴安娜王妃的肖像取而代之。

这个主意也许不算太荒谬。整个90年代出现了一种现象，这种现象又是取自小报新闻业的三流做法，即把公众的自白和功能失常行为处理成"现实"娱乐的假象。这种趋势也在电视上表现出来，比如"大众事实性节目"或者"真人秀"，这类节目和50年代那些廉价的"剥削"电影没什么区别，都是以所谓对过失行为或耸人听闻行为的教育研究来娱乐观众。

在90年代，戴安娜事件在大众媒体里被定位成了一个完美的"故事"——一位皇室成员，年轻、富有魅力以及并不幸福的婚姻。媒体对公众人物自白的需求在日渐增加，并且随着新闻业对个人隐私和人身创伤的报道占据绝大部分版面（这样的趋势在翠西·艾敏的作品里反映出来），戴安娜生活中的关系和一举一动都像现实生活肥皂剧一样被展示在报纸上。戴安娜自己也对这种狂热起了推波助澜的作用，她答应在公开访谈节目中露面，由BBC电视台于1995年11月进行摄制和广播。（令人觉得怪异的巧合是，这个访谈之后的节目是首次播放甲壳虫乐队"新"单曲"像鸟一样自由"的音乐电视，已故约翰·列侬的声音从老唱片中通过数字技术手段被加进这部音乐电视里。）

戴安娜的"真实生活"剧最终以王妃在车祸中丧生的悲剧性结局而落下帷幕，车祸的发生是由于一些花边新闻记者不顾一切在后面追车所造成的，因为他们想要拍到戴安娜和她的男友多狄·法耶德的照片，法耶德是伦敦著名哈罗德百货公司那位直率老板的儿子。从符号学的角度来说，戴安娜转换成为当代社会和文化的模式，立刻变成一种死亡崇拜。全民哀悼的壮观景象令美国作家格里·维多不禁感慨道："我实在不明白为什么你们这些人为自己感到如此难过。"他的意思是，戴安娜之死表达了世纪末民族绝望和病态情绪的潜流。(vii)

vi

"感觉：萨奇收藏的英国青年艺术家作品"
皇家艺术学院，伦敦
1997年9月18日至12月28日
画廊导览
封面设计：Why Not Associates设计公司

"Sensation: Young British Artists from the Saatchi Collection"
Royal Academy of Arts, London
18 September -28 December 1997
Gallery Guide
Cover design: Why Not Associates

Given the efficiency with which these early works by 'Young British Artists' attracted attention, controversy and power brokerage by a patrician class to whom the workings of artisan popular culture were wholly exotic, it was fitting that their first serious collector would be the advertising mogul Charles Saatchi, whose clients in the 1980s had included the Conservative party. In 1997, the exhibition of works from his collection, "Sensation: Young British Artists from the Saatchi Collection", would attract some 3,000 visitors per day to the Royal Academy of Arts, London (vi). The exhibition was distinguished by the manner in which many of the works on display appeared gratuitously fixated on violent death.

In many ways, the principal cultural themes of the 1990s would seem to converge in the tragic figure of Diana, Princess of Wales, who died in a sensational car accident in Paris in August, 1997. It was even suggested by one journalist that a photograph of Diana should have replaced the controversial portrait of the child murderer Myra Hindley as the central exhibit in the "Sensation" exhibition.

And this was perhaps not such a ridiculous idea. Throughout the 1990s, there had been the phenomenon - again derived from the worst aspects of tabloid journalism - of treating public confession and dysfunctional behaviour as a spurious form of 'reality' entertainment. The trend in television for what was known as 'Popular Factual Programming' - or 'reality TV' - was for the most part nothing more than a return to the sleazy 'exploitation' films of the 1950s, in which audiences were titillated by supposedly educational studies of delinquent or lurid behaviour.

In Diana, the populist media of the 1990s identified the perfect 'story' - a Royal figure, young, attractive and unhappily married. As the media's hunger for public confession increased, with journalism becoming dominated by public accounts of private and personal trauma (a trend that would be reflected in the art of Tracey Emin), so Diana's relationships and activities were played out in the newspapers like a real-life soap opera. Diana fuelled this obsession herself, by agreeing to appear on a public interview, filmed by BBC television and broadcast in November, 1995. (By eerie co-incidence, this interview would precede the first showing of a video for a 'new' single by The Beatles - *Free As A Bird* - in which the voice of the dead John Lennon was digitally added to the track from old recordings.)

The tragic concluding episode of Diana's 'real life' drama would be the death of the Princess in a car that was being chased by 'paparazzi' journalists, desperate to obtain photographs of Diana with her boyfriend, Dodi Fayed, the son of the outspoken owner of the famous Harrods department store in London. Transposed semiotically into the patterning of contemporary society and culture, Diana became an instant death cult. The extravagant displays of public mourning prompted the American writer, Gore Vidal, to remark: "I had no idea that you people were so sorry for yourselves." What he meant was that the death of Diana had served to give expression to a fin de siècle undercurrent of national despair and sentimental morbidity (vii).

就在"感觉"展在皇家艺术学院举办的同时，英国泰特美术馆也举办了名为"罗塞蒂、伯纳·琼斯和华兹的年代——英国象征主义1860–1910"的维多利亚晚期艺术展 (viii)。就如作家菲利普·豪尔在对展览进行评论时所指出的，这两个世纪末的展览具有明显的相似之处，其作品都是以死亡、臆想、病态、性欲和融合为中心主题，讲述的都是这样一个时代，即都市的奢侈和纯粹的审美魅力以心理学家荣格所说的"阴影"方式表达出来，即他们所处时代的阴暗和不稳定的潜意识。

在这些展览里，暴力、病态和死亡意象似乎预言着即将临近的战争、灾难和国际创伤时期。对于维多利亚时代晚期而言，它们预示的是第一次世界大战。而对于"英国青年艺术"的创作者们来说，它们预示的是2001年9月恐怖分子对纽约世贸中心的袭击，以及紧接其后的"反恐战争"。

vii

威尔士王妃的葬礼照片
1997年9月
©摄影师

Photograph of Funeral of Princess of Wales
September 1997
© the photographer

At the same time that "Sensation" was held at the Royal Academy, there was an exhibition of late Victorian art at Tate Britain entitled "The Age of Rosetti, Burne-Jones and Watts - Symbolism in Britain 1860-1910" (viii). As the writer Philip Hoare pointed out in his review of the exhibition, there was a marked similarity between these two exhibitions of fin de siècle art. Both contained works in which death, somnambulance, morbidity, sexual desire and deliquescence were central themes. Both seemed to speak of a time when metropolitan luxury and sheer aesthetic gorgeousness were being expressed in terms of what the psychologist Karl Jung called the 'shadow' - the dark, volatile sub-consciousness of their times.

For in both of these exhibitions, the violence, morbidity and imagery of death seemed to prophesy some approaching period of war, disaster and international trauma. For the late Victorians, this would be the First World War. For the creators of 'Young British Art', it would be the terrorist attack on the World Trade Center, New York in September 2001, and the ensuing 'War on Terror'.

viii

亨利·佩格荣
Sibylla Fatidica
1904
大理石
162.5cm×122.5cm×111 cm
©泰特，伦敦，2006

Henry Pegram
Sibylla Fatidica
1904
Marble
162.5cm×122.5cm×111 cm
© Tate, London 2006

皮力
PILI

从"吉尔伯特和乔治"1993年在中国美术馆举办的展览开始，到现在已经整整13年了。当年，吉尔伯特和乔治的展览举办的时候，中国的艺术院校并不教授表现主义之后的艺术，我们对于当代主义的了解通常是来自于那些廉价印刷的黑白图片和并非准确的翻译。大部分中国艺术家和批评家也都是在这种误读中开始了自己的当代艺术实验。所以，这些并不难解释为什么中国当代艺术在1980到1990迅速地重演了一遍西方现代艺术史。作为好奇的年轻人，当时的年轻艺术家莫名其妙地崇拜任何和社会现实主义不同的作品，从来不考虑其背后的观念和它们作为艺术品的基本要求。"吉尔伯特和乔治"的展览是我们这代人第一次看到西方当代艺术的原作。无法形容在知识闭塞的情况下作为年轻的艺术家看到这些作品时获得的视觉上的震撼，他们和那些所谓的"观念"的艺术之间形成了剧烈的对比。

虽然是一个官方的文化交流项目，"吉尔伯特和乔治"的展览当时在相对封闭的社会上获得的反响是不能和今天在北京、上海和广州开幕的任何一个当代艺术展览相比的，但是从另一角度说，"吉尔伯特和乔治"的展览在某个方面又是影响深远的。它们在某种程度上，催生了上个世纪90年代在北京东村发生的观念艺术和行为艺术，激发了比玩世现实主义和政治波普更加年青的一代艺术家。

中国的当代艺术诞生于80年代，诞生于后印象派和表现主义的传统中，这两种风格和中国流行的现实主义绘画有着很强的内在关联。虽然，80年代的时候，劳申柏在中国举办了一次展览，但是当时中国社会对于二战以后的当代艺术尚未译介过来，中国社会和文化还在一个从抽象的文化政治角度反思历史的阶段，所以他的艺术并没有造成广泛的影响。而吉尔伯特和乔治作为英国80年代艺术的代表被介绍到中国来，当时中国艺术的背景已经发生了变化。

首先是80年代以来的以绘画为主导的中国前卫艺术已经被简化为玩世现实主义和政治波普的绘画，而这种单一的绘画形式在冷战结束后成为国际收藏界追捧的对象；其次，经历了80年代末期的短暂政治风波后，90年代的中国社会从政治的封闭化迅速走向全面的"市场经济化"，虽然不能简单地说已经在本质上"西方化"，但是社会生活的内涵发生了巨大的变化，无论是文化还是生活，人们对抽象意识形态并不再感兴趣，而是开始追逐消费社会的生活乐趣。"吉尔伯特和乔治"的展览就是在这种背景下被介绍进来的，并影响到了在北京的年轻反叛的中国艺术家正在进行的观念艺术与行为艺术的试验。 他们的展览刷新了尚在物质贫乏阶段的中国当代艺术对"视觉"、"质量"的理解。 和这个相关， 他们颠倒了，而不是打破了艺术和生活之间的界限，并在不断地延长和强化这种错位(ix)。 他们生活方式和艺术作品之间的关系以及某种对于日常生活的极端性的表现也影响了中国艺术家。

It has been thirteen years since Gilbert & George exhibited at the National Art Museum of China in 1993. At the time of that exhibition, art academies in China did not teach art history beyond Expressionism, so our understanding of contemporary art usually came from cheaply printed black and white photographs and inaccurate translations. Most Chinese artists and critics inevitably began their own experiments in contemporary art from such misinterpretations, therefore it is not difficult to explain why Chinese contemporary art between 1980 and 1990 was a rapid replay of Western modern art history. As curious youth, the young contemporary artists of the time inexplicably worshipped any work that was different from social-realism without considering the ideas behind these works or their basic requirements as works of art. The Gilbert & George exhibition marked the first occasion our generation saw original works of contemporary Western art. It is impossible to describe the visual shock young artists living under intellectual censorship experienced in seeing these works. They formed a fierce contrast to so-called 'conceptual' art.

Despite being a governmental cultural exchange project, the reactions elicited by the Gilbert & George exhibition, in a time when society was closed off, cannot be compared to any contemporary art exhibition opening in Beijing, Shanghai or Guangzhou today. It had a profound and far-reaching impact. In some ways it can be said that the works hastened the advent of conceptual and performance art in the East Village in Beijing during the 1990s and inspired the generation which followed the painting movements of 'Cynical Realism' and 'Political Pop'.

Chinese contemporary art came into being in the 1980s, in the midst of an academic vogue for Post-Impressionist and Expressionist traditions. These two styles were strongly related to the social-realist painting style then popular in China. Although an exhibition of works by Robert Rauschenberg was held in China in the 1980s, Chinese society at that time did not come to understand post-war contemporary art. The country was still in a period of rethinking history through an abstract cultural-political perspective, and so the exhibition did not wield extensive influence. But by the time the works of Gilbert & George were introduced to China as representative of British art of the 1980s, a change had already taken place in the Chinese art scene.

First, the avant-garde painting which had come into existence since the 1980s had already been simplified as either 'Cynical Realism' or 'Political Pop'. These monotonous forms of painting became highly sought after by collectors in the post Cold War period. Next, following brief political turmoil at the end of the 1980s, Chinese society in the 1990s went from being sealed off politically towards rapid market economic development. Whilst we cannot simply say that it had already been 'Westernised', the content of social life had undergone huge transformations. Whether cultural or lifestyle, people were no longer interested in abstract ideology but rather in pursuing the daily pleasures of consumer society. It was against this backdrop that the Gilbert & George exhibition was introduced and influenced the conceptual and performance art that young and rebellious contemporary Beijing artists were then experimenting with. Under the existing period of material poverty, the exhibition restored contemporary Chinese artists' understanding of 'visual' and 'quality'. Gilbert & George appeared to invert, not destroy, the boundaries between art and life, and consistently extended and emphasised this dislocation (ix). The relationship between their lifestyle and art, as well as giving expression to the extremies of daily life, also influenced Chinese artists.

ix

吉尔伯特和乔治
死亡 希望 生命 恐惧
1984
四联画
422cm×250cm, 422cm×652cm, 422cm×250cm, 422cm×652cm
© 吉尔伯特和乔治

Gilbert & George
DEATH HOPE LIFE FEAR
1984
Four Part Picture
422cm×250cm, 422cm×652cm, 422cm×250cm, 422cm×652cm
© Gilbert & George

当时的中国艺术界并没有很多人知道，在这个展览在中国开幕的同时，由吉尔伯特和乔治催生的另一场革命正在英国发生，并形成主流。这就是"YBA现象"[Young British Artist]。如果说吉尔伯特和乔治疏通了观念艺术和日常生活之间的渠道，让艺术获得了日常生活的视觉形式，那么更年青的一代艺术家则是顺应社会的变革，一方面延续观念艺术对于现实的思考，另一方面让艺术变得更加具有不啻于现实的视觉魅力。 也正是因此，他们成为20世纪以来，曝光最多和被媒体追捧的当代艺术。应该说，在大众传媒的作用下他们使得艺术从被大众排斥的东西转变为被人们关注的东西。其实YBA引人注目还有更深层的艺术史上的背景。

流行文化和大众传媒对于当代艺术的挑战不仅仅在于文化姿态和价值判断，同时也表现在艺术的语言方式和呈现方式上。流行文化以电影电视、音乐、游戏等手段，能在一个时间段内调动所有人的感觉能力，甚至能产生虚拟和仿真的效果，所有的这些都是传统艺术在欣赏中很难提供给观众的。同样，艺术如何在美丽的现实生活中获得自己存在的理由和价值？这是后现代主义留给艺术的最大问题。传统艺术媒介的界限没有了，装置、录像、行为都体现出艺术开始借助观众身体性和心理性的参与来获得自己的价值。的确，后现代主义在几十年的发展中，使艺术从形式和媒介的囚笼中解脱出来，使之获得更大的空间。但是，这还不足以证明艺术在今天的价值和理由。事实上，无论是波依斯还是汉斯·哈克，无论他们的精神多么鼓舞人，对于很多人来说它一方面不能显示出艺术的特性，一方面又过于冷漠、概念化、晦涩和教条。

正是在这个背景下，英国年轻艺术家的努力才显得如此引人注目。1997年在英国伦敦的皇家艺术学院举办了名为"感觉"的展览，一批年轻的艺术家浮现出来（这也是YBA这个词的由来）。这里包括达明安·赫斯特[Damien Hirst]、马克·奎安[Marc Quinn]、翠西·艾敏[Tracey Emin]和瑞查·怀特里德[Rachel Whiteread]。达明安·赫斯特直接使用肉体作为作品的材料，在《母子分离》[Mother and Child Divided，1993] (x)中，他将动物劈成若干个截面，然后用漂亮的盒子安装起来；或者《一千年》[A Thousand Years，1990]中，用腐烂的肉来培养苍蝇和蛆。从中，我们体会到的是对于生命过程的检验，以及对于欲望的反省。马克·奎安将自己的血凝固，然后做成自己的头像(xi)，或者用化学材料做出极端写实的被剥去皮肤的人。翠西·艾敏的作品就像她的自传，她将过去32年和她同床过的人的名字和书信贴在展厅的帐篷里，所有的这些似乎成为一个隐喻，她就是那帐篷，而每个名字就像伤口一样布满了帐篷(xii)。瑞查·怀特里德的作品相当简单，她用日常物体的负空间来构成自己的作品。她将蜡、水泥、肥皂或者塑料注入物体自身的空间中，然后将其凝固，比如《房子》[House，1993]（1994年被毁坏了），一个伦敦东区维多利亚式房子内部空间的模子制成的水泥作品(xiii)，这样，她将一个可以被感觉到的空间呈现为一个视觉实体。

x

达明安·赫斯特
母体分离
1993
钢，GPR合成物，玻璃，硅树脂密封胶，母牛，小牛，甲醛溶液
两个容器：190cm×322.5cm×109cm
另外两个容器：102.9cm×168.9cm×62.3cm
Jay Jopling/伦敦白色立方画廊借予展出
© 艺术家
照片：Stephen White

Damien Hirst
Mother and Child Divided
1993
Steel, GRP composites, glass, silicone sealant,
cow, calf and formaldehyde solution
2 tanks: 190cm×322.5cm×109cm / 2 tanks:
102.9cm×168.9cm×62.3cm
Courtesy Jay Jopling/ White Cube, London
© the artist
Photo: Stephen White

xii

翠西·艾敏
所有和我睡过的人 1963-1995
1995
刺绣的帐篷，床垫，灯
122cm×245cm×215cm
Jay Jopling/伦敦白色立方画廊借予展出
© 艺术家
照片：Stephen White

Tracey Emin
Everyone I Have Ever Slept With 1963-1995
1995
Appliquéd tent, mattress and light
122cm×245cm×215cm
Courtesy Jay Jopling/ White Cube, London
© the artist
Photo: Stephen White

At the time, few people in the Chinese contemporary art world realised that, concurrent with the opening of their exhibition in China, Gilbert & George had hastened the advent of another revolution in Britain which was soon to become mainstream. This was the 'YBA' (Young British Artist) phenomenon of the 1990s. If Gilbert & George combined art and life, allowing art to take on the visual forms of daily life, then a younger generation of artists complied with this social transformation, on the one hand continuing conceptual art's reflection of reality, and on the other hand allowing art to possess visual glamour. It is precisely because of this that they became the most highly exposed contemporary artists of the late twentieth century. It can be said that through mass media, art was transformed from something rejected by the masses into something to be looked at, though there is also a deeper art historical background that explains the attention the 'YBA's aroused.

The challenge that popular culture and mainstream media present to contemporary art rests not only in cultural stance and value judgment, but also in the linguistic approach and presentation of art. Popular culture uses film, television, music, video games, mobile phones, and so forth to stir people's perceptions within a period of time, sometimes producing artificial and false results. All of this provides the masses with something very difficult to come by when viewing and appreciating traditional art. Similarly, how does art acquire its reason for existence and value from the beauty of real life? This is the biggest question postmodernism has left us with. The traditional boundaries between artistic media no longer exist. Installation, video and performance all show that art is beginning to garner value by drawing support from audiences' physical and psychological participation. Indeed, the past few decades of postmodern development have liberated artists from the prison of form and medium, allowing them greater freedom. But this is not enough to demonstrate the value and reason of art today. Whether it is Joseph Beuys or Hans Haacke, no matter how inspiring their spirit is, to many people their work does not reveal the unique qualities of art, appearing instead as overly detached, conceptual, obscure, and dogmatic.

It was precisely against this backdrop that an emergent group of young British artists caught the public's attention in 1997 in the exhibition "Sensation", held at the Royal Academy of Arts in London. Amongst others, the exhibition included the artists Damien Hirst, Marc Quinn, Tracey Emin, and Rachel Whiteread . Damien Hirst used the body as the material for his works. In works such as *Mother and Child Divided*, 1993, he sliced up animals and placed them in beautiful formaldehyde-filled cases(x). In *A Thousand Years*, 1990, the artist fed a cow's rotting head to flies and maggots. Both examples display an examination of the life process and an introspective meditation on desire. In *Self*, 1991, Marc Quinn made a sculpture of his head from a coagulated block of his own blood(xi). Tracey Emin's work *Everyone I Have Ever Slept With 1963-1995*, 1995 is autobiographical, like many of her works. Here she embroidered the names of all the people she had slept with on the inside of a large blue tent(xii). Metaphorically, she is the tent and each name is a wound covering the entire tent. Rachel Whiteread's works are simple and often integrate domestic objects. She fills the empty or negative spaces with wax, cement, resin or plastic. For example, *House*, 1993 (destroyed in 1994) was a concrete cast of the interior of an entire Victorian terraced house in the East End of London(xiii). The artist transformed an invisible yet palpable space into a visual entity.

xi

马克·奎安
自我
1991
血，不锈钢，塑胶，制冷剂
208cm×63cm×63 cm
Jay Jopling/伦敦白色立方画廊借予展出
© 艺术家
照片：Stephen White

Marc Quinn
Self
1991
Blood, stainless steel, perspecm × and refrigeration equipment
208cm×63cm×63 cm
Courtesy Jay Jopling/ White Cube, London
© the artist
Photo: Stephen White

　　所有的作品似乎都提供了一种简单的传达观念的方式，同时它也将艺术的重心从抽象的政治和道德转向了个体在现场的体验，从宣扬艺术家的观念转向期待观众的心理判断。它们强制性地将观众和作品的心理距离拉近。但所有的这些作品形式相当简单和静止，甚至符合传统雕塑的视觉样式。从某种程度上看，它们是刺激的。但艺术家又将这种刺激控制在一个有效的限度之中。他们将血腥、伤害、破坏这些残酷的事实包装得漂漂亮亮的，展现在观众面前。但是它又不失时机地暗示观众漂亮下面的东西。对于很多人来说，这些作品真正体现了艺术在今天的理由和方式。它们出现在画廊里，这是一个不同于漆黑的剧院和封闭的书房的公共环境，人们失去了私人空间中的自由感。作品将社会禁忌、心理禁忌以美丽的形式交给你的时候，又让你无法掩饰自己的观点和羞怯。于是，所有微妙的感觉出现了。它将观众的注意力引向那些难以捕捉的现实，从中观众看到了正面和负面的感觉。它提供了一种新看待身体和隐私的角度，那些本应是私下才可看到的东西，现在会使观众坐卧不安。对于艺术而言，他们的作品似乎提供了一种新方式，使观众有机会感觉当今的很多幻想。人的触觉、嗅觉、视觉、听觉、味觉都在这里真实却又含蓄地发生着作用。

　　如果说装置的出现意味着艺术的一种努力，即试图诱使观众参与到作品中来，使观众产生一种不同于流行文化、日常生活和科学技术所提供的特殊体验，并由此证明艺术在今天存在的价值，那么《感觉》则轻而易举地实现了这一点。而实现这一点的秘密在于，他们从日常生活中提炼出感觉，并期待观众再次感觉这种感觉，而不是像以前的观念艺术那样，用艺术内部的概念来笼罩和改造感觉。假定在当代艺术中，YBA有什么突破的话，那这个突破就是将身体性和切身体验作为她的特有武器加以使用，从而证明自己的存在和合理的努力。这就像瑞查·怀特里德的雕塑，她把那些实际存在却为我们视而不见的感觉变成一个实体，让我们无法回避。

　　虽然到90年代末，YBA就已经从杂志和画册上被介绍到中国来了，而《感觉》的画册也是很多中国年轻艺术家的必读书之一，但是除了有机会去国外的艺术家以外，很少有人能看到这些作品的原作。然而，尽管YBA的艺术直到今天才能来中国展览，但是其影响却是早就在中国扩散开了。在2000年一个由栗宪庭策划的"对伤害的迷恋"的展览上，6位年轻的艺术家分别使用了人和动物的尸体、血液、脂肪油，采用肢解、并置的形式，来完成了他们的作品。这些作品展出以后，引起了巨大的震动。遗憾的是，由于中国社会的特殊现状，关于这个展览的讨论并没有在学术层面上公开展开。栗宪庭先生对于"尸体现象"的出现，做了自己的分析。他认为这些作品和中国社会有着密切的关系，同时也暗含有对东西方社会道德的双向挑战的意味。而艺术界的同行则将其理解为一种为名利场逻辑驱使的不择手段。其实"尸体现象"的出现集中反映了中国艺术现象的内在问题。

xiii

瑞查·怀特里德
房子
1993
混合媒体
艺术家和高古轩画廊
相片：Sue Ormerod

Rachel Whiteread
House
1993
Mixed media
Courtesy of the artist and Gagosian Gallery
Photo: Sue Ormerod

All these works seem to present a simple transmission of ideas. At the same time they shift the focus of art from abstract politics and ethics to the individual onsite experience, and from propagating artists' ideas to looking towards the audience for a psychological response. They emphasise closing the psychological gap between the audience and the art. Yet, all of these works are simple and static, they are, in fact, similar to the visual forms of traditional sculpture. From a certain perspective, they are provocative, but the artists control this provocation within an effective limit. They use blood and injury to destroy brutal realities, packaging them beautifully and exhibiting them before the audience. The works hint at what lies beneath the beauty. To many people, these works show the true reason and method of art today. Galleries present a different and dark public setting, where works are presented as social and psychological taboos, but deny people the ability to conceal their reactions. Consequently, subtleties of feeling are revealed. The works lead audiences toward inapprehensible realities and provide a more nuanced art experience. The exposure of conventionally private things does not sit well with audiences, it provides a new perspective on the corporeal and the private. These works have provided the audience with a new way of perceiving contemporary fantasies. People's sense of touch, smell, sight, hearing and taste are all called upon and truly embody the role of the initiator.

If the emergence of the power of installation signifies an effort on the part of art, namely the attempt to draw audiences into a work and thus generating a unique experience distinct from daily life, and therefore proving the value of art's existence today, then "Sensation" realised this effortlessly. The secret to realising this lies in the way the artists extract feelings from daily life and look to audiences to re-live these feelings, unlike concepts of the past which relied on art's internal ideologies to envelop and transform feelings. If the 'YBAs' made any breakthroughs in contemporary art, it was through the use of corporeality, as well as the cutting off of corporeality, thus proving its own reason for existence and rationality. This can be likened to Rachel Whiteread's sculptures, in which she transforms an existing yet invisible feeling into an unavoidable entity.

Although the 'YBAs' had already been introduced to China via magazines and catalogues by the late 1990s, and the "Sensation" catalogue had become a 'must-read' for many young Chinese artists, apart from those who could leave the country, very few people were able to view the works in their original form. While it is now that the 'YBAs' are exhibiting in China for the first time, their influence nonetheless spread throughout the country a long time ago. In 2000, Li Xianting curated an exhibition entitled "Infatuation with Injury" featuring six young artists whose works incorporated dismembered and reworked human and animal corpses, blood, and oil extracted from fat. These works caused public uproar. Regretfully, due to the unique status quo of Chinese society, discussions regarding this exhibition were never developed and made public on an educational level. Li Xianting made his own analysis of the 'corpse phenomenon.' He thought that these works were closely related to Chinese society's deeper unrest, simultaneously implying a two-way challenge to both Western and Eastern social morals. As for the art world, some interpreted it as a shameless stunt to gain fame and recognition, nonetheless, the 'corpse phenomenon' collectively reflected the problems of Chinese art at that moment.

在震动之后 / After the Shock

1999年，邱志杰和吴美纯策划了"后感性"，这个展览是一个大规模的观念艺术的展览，展览涉及了当代艺术各个方面的媒介和观点("对伤害的迷恋"的艺术家也是出自于这个展览)。仅从展览的名字，我们就能体会到英国的"感觉"展览对于中国当代艺术家的影响。问题可以变得很简单，为什么只有"感觉"这个展览会对中国当代艺术产生如此巨大的影响，而同时其他的展览没有这样的作用呢？为什么达明安·赫斯特的作品能变异成这样？原因在于中国并没有一个有效接受外部信息的输入渠道，所有关于西方当代艺术的知识并不是通过学校的传授，通过媒体的客观介绍，或者艺术家在海外留学获得的，而是来源于口碑相传，来源于老艺术家偶尔带回来的几本画册。每一期的外国美术刊物来了，年轻的艺术家往往只能从几个平方厘米的图片上获得仅有的信息，他们甚至不能阅读文字。中国艺术家在开始当代艺术创作之前很少能看到原作。这就是中国艺术家的困境，年轻的艺术家在不了解原作的情况下，正在预支那些没有价值的"自由"以及在各种媒体传播和陈述中变异和沉浮的"观念"。

"余震"是我的同事、也是这个展览的发起人和策划人之一秦思源去年2月我们在伦敦考察的时候，想起的名字。当时展览的方向还是设定在展览YBA以后的艺术家。他的意思是YBA是英国社会20世纪90年代的一个shock［震动］，而我们试图展示在这个"震动之后"[aftershock]的东西。但是随着我们的走访和策划，我们还是选择了一个以YBA为主的展览，其目的在于重新梳理和还原一个现象。我们保留了"余震"这个名字，因为艺术总是长江后浪推前浪，吉尔伯特和乔治在80年代就开始引起英国公众的兴趣，YBA也可以被看做一次余震。

YBA已经在当代艺术领域成为一个新闻的"噱头"，其发展也映射了我们对于艺术在传媒笼罩的当代社会中的真正位置更加深入的思考，我们觉得这个展览对中国当代艺术发展还是有相当启示作用的。今天的中国正在经历着英国艺术在十年前经历的东西：火热但是态度保守而投机的艺术市场泡沫，热情但是浅薄的大众传媒，保守的美术馆与激烈的艺术革新等等。英国的青年艺术家在这个背景下创造了一个传奇，也似乎宿命似的同样面临着体制化、市场化和浅薄化的危机。21世纪以来中国当代艺术正在成为传媒和市场追捧的焦点，这无疑是对一个转型社会的震动，但是在这个震动之后，我们是否能走出一条不同而更加宽广的路呢？我想这是在"余震"中我们应该思考的问题。

In 1999, Qiu Zhijie and Wu Meichun curated "Post-Sense Sensibility", a large-scale conceptual art exhibition, involving every medium and point of view in contemporary art (the artists of "Infatuation with Injury" were also drawn from this exhibition). From the name alone, we can understand the influence that "Sensation" had on Chinese contemporary art. The question can be put simply: why did "Sensation" have such a huge influence on Chinese contemporary art when other exhibitions did not? The reason lies in the fact that China does not have an effective receiving channel for outside information. Knowledge of contemporary Western art did not come from the classroom, objective media reporting or artists' overseas experience, but from word of mouth, public praise and a few catalogues older artists might occasionally bring back from their travels. With the arrival of each foreign art publication, young artists had but a few square-centimetre images to pore over for the little information they offered. They may not have been able to read the text. Very few Chinese artists could see original works prior to creating their own art. This is the difficult position Chinese artists faced. Without understanding the original works, young artists drew advances on the worthless 'freedom' and 'concept' that has been propagated by every form of media, ever-changing in meaning.

"Aftershock" was the name I came up with in consultation with Colin Chinnery, the exhibition's initiator and co-curator, when we were researching in London. At the time, the direction of the exhibition was still aimed at showing art from Britain post 'YBA', the idea being that the work of the 'YBA' period represented a shock to British society in the 1990s and we were attempting to reveal the 'aftershock.' But during the planning stages, we chose to present an exhibition which focused on art of the 'YBA' generation, the objective being to reflect on and reassess this phenomenon. We kept the name "Aftershock" because art is always the "back tide of the Yangtze River pushing the front tide." If Gilbert & George began to draw the attention of the wider British public in the 1980s, the 'YBAs' can then be considered an 'aftershock'.

The 'YBA' generation became newsworthy within the contemporary art world and beyond, especially in expanding and shedding light on a deeper reflection of art's true role in our media saturated society, and we feel that this exhibition will fulfill an equally enlightening function for Chinese contemporary art. Today in China artists are undergoing a situation similar to that in Britain ten years ago: a heated but attitudinally conservative and speculative art market bubble, accompanied by enthusiastic but superficial mass media, conservative art galleries and museums, and intense artistic innovation. Against this backdrop, the 'Young British Artists' produced a legendary and seemingly predestined crisis that came from their being simultaneously institutionalised, commodified and trivialised. Since the beginning of the present century, Chinese contemporary art has been the focal point for mass media and the market. This is undoubtedly a shock for a transitional society, but, after this shock, will we be able to pave a different and wider road? I think this is an issue we should consider with "Aftershock".

杰克·查普曼和迪诺斯·查普曼
Jake and Dinos Chapman

翠西·艾敏
Tracey Emin

道格拉斯·戈登
Douglas Gordon

莫娜·哈透姆
Mona Hatoum

达明安·赫斯特
Damien Hirst

加里·休姆
Gary Hume

莎拉·卢卡斯
Sarah Lucas

马克·奎安
Marc Quinn

山姆·泰勒-伍德
Sam Taylor-Wood

马克·渥林格
Mark Wallinger

吉莉安·韦英
Gillian Wearing

杰克・查普曼和迪诺斯・查普曼
Jake and Dinos Chapman

杰克·查普曼和迪诺斯·查普曼
Jay Jopling / 伦敦白色立方画廊
摄影：Anna Schori

Jake and Dinos Chapman
Courtesy Jay Jopling/White Cube, London
Photo: Anna Schori

杰克·查普曼和迪诺斯·查普曼 / Jake and Dinos Chapman

杰克·查普曼和迪诺斯·查普曼，分别于1966年和1962年出生在切尔滕纳姆和伦敦。1990年，两人毕业于皇家艺术学院，获美学硕士学位，此后开始共同创作。如今在伦敦生活和创作。

1993年，通过展览"战争的灾难"[The Disasters of War]，查普曼兄弟进入公众视线。18世纪西班牙艺术家戈雅创作的法西拿破仑战争的著名系列版画，使查普曼兄弟深受启发，他们运用塑料模型再现了这一历史画面。2003年，伦敦泰特美术馆举行的他们的特纳奖提名展里，作品《变本加厉》[Insult to Injury] 延续了这位西班牙艺术家对他们的影响。

查普曼兄弟着迷于一种粗犷的风格，通过他们的作品对恐怖和卑贱的道德边缘进行了探索。1996年，他们的展览"查普曼世界"[Chapmanworld] 在当代艺术学院引起了很大争议，原因是他们当时展出了名为《悲惨的人体》[Tragic Anatomies] 的作品，这一作品采用不寻常的手法对儿童模型进行了变形。

不过，在对待沉重的主题时，这对兄弟常使用的是一种特别的并且违反常理的幽默手法。2002年，在伦敦白色立方画廊举办的"查普曼家族收藏作品展"上[Works from the Chapman Family Collection]，他们展出了一些雕塑作品。这些雕塑一眼望去是非洲和大洋洲的古代宗教雕塑，但近距离观察就会发现都是"赝品"。确实，雕塑身上，时空错乱地使用了全球性人公司的标志，如麦当劳。展出是严肃的，像文物一般，但艺术家的作品却是对现代资本主义荒谬形象的嘲讽。除了这些雕塑外，还有一系列用相同名字命名的巨大而细腻的素描作品。其中，《查普曼家族收藏－素描III》[Drawing III from the Chapman Family Collection, 2002]，展示了一个在十字架上摆放着的"巨无霸"汉堡头像，批判新自由主义和基督民主政治的种种所谓道德。

查普曼兄弟永无止境的讽刺和幽默伴随着他们的个展历程，展览包括："迪诺斯 查普曼和杰克 查普曼，GCSE 艺术考试"[GCSE Art Exam]，艺术银座空间，东京，2000年；"杰克 查普曼和迪诺斯 查普曼，新作"[New Work]，现代艺术馆，伦敦，2001年；"被强暴的创造力"[The Rape of Creativity]，牛津现代艺术馆，2003年；"向恐龙解释基督徒"[Explaining Christians to Dinosaurs]，波坚思美术馆，2005年；以及2005年在白色立方画廊举办的"像狗一样回味自己的呕吐物"[Like a dog returns to its vomit]。利物浦泰特美术馆已经筹划了2006-2007年查普曼兄弟大型作品回顾展。

查普曼兄弟的作品曾在许多重要的群体展上展出，比如"感觉：萨奇收藏的英国青年艺术家作品"[Sensation: Young British Artists from the Saatchi Collection]，伦敦、柏林和纽约，1997-1999年；还有"'精彩!'来自伦敦的新艺术"，明尼阿波利斯和休斯敦，1995-1996年。就是在这一展览中，公众开始观看他们的雕塑——《超级人物》[Ubermensch，1995]。这个雕塑做的是史蒂芬·霍金——英国著名的物理学家和数学家坐在轮椅上，在悬崖顶摇摇欲坠的样子，颇像埃德文·兰德希尔的《峡谷中的君主》[Monarch of the Glenn，1851]。这里，霍金的形象被丑化了，尽管他有着"超人类"的智慧和地位，作品中他濒临危险的处境突出了他那孱弱的身体。尽管这位科学家提出了很多著名模式，如"无边界条件"理论，即宇宙是有限的，但是在假想的时间里没有边界这样的理论，可是这件作品，提醒我们的是他同样也要面对死亡。

近期，他们的作品因为某些悲剧性事件的发生而再度引起公众注意。作品《地狱》[Hell]在2004年受到了毁坏，可以说，这是他们迄今为止最重要的雕塑作品，曾于2000年在英国皇家艺术学院的伦敦"天启"展[Apocalypse]上展出。不过，他们并没有灰心，而是在继续关注重大事件并在吸取别人独特之处的基础上，继续创造着大量的新作品。

参考阅读：
"Jake & Dinos Chapman. Works from the Chapman Family Collection"， Suhail Malik撰文，Jay Jopling/伦敦白色立方画廊，2002年
"Jake & Dinos Chapman"， Eckhard Schneider, Jack Chapman, James Hall和Rudolf Sagmeister编写，奥地利波坚思美术馆，2005年
"Jake and Dinos Chapman"，泰特出版社，伦敦，2006年

Jake and Dinos Chapman, born respectively in Cheltenham, 1966 and London, 1962, have worked collaboratively since they graduated in 1990 with a Fine Art MA from the Royal College of Art, London. They live and work in London.

The Chapmans came to public attention in 1993 with The Disasters of War exhibition. Using plastic model figurines, the brothers recreated a series of tableaux inspired by the eighteenth century artist Francisco Goya's famous series of etchings of the Franco-Spanish Napoleonic wars. This fascination with the Spanish artist has continued with their *Insult to Injury* series included in their Turner Prize nomination exhibition in 2003 at Tate, London.

Jake and Dinos Chapman are fascinated by the vulgar, and their work explores the moral boundaries of horror and the abject. In 1996, their exhibition "Chapmanworld" caused controversy at the Institute of Contemporary Arts, London as it featured works entitled *Tragic Anatomies*, or grotesquely deformed mannequins of children.

Nonetheless, the brothers always bring a particular and often perverse humour to their exploration of heavy themes. Their exhibition "Works from the Chapman Family Collection" at White Cube gallery, London in 2002 included what appeared to be ancient sacred African and Oceanic sculptures, but which on closer inspection turned out to be 'counterfeits'. Indeed, the sculptures anachronistically bear the logos of global corporation such as McDonalds. Here the works are solemnly displayed, like relics, yet they are offered up by the artists as absurd anti-effigies to modern capitalism. The sculptures were complemented by a series of meticulously drafted large prints bearing the same name. *Drawing III from the Chapman Family Collection* (2002) shows a 'Big Mac' hamburger head offered up on a crucifix, as a tongue in cheek critique of the morals of Neo-Liberalism and Christian Democracy.

The Chapmans' solo exhibition history also bears the traces of their restless burlesque humour. Exhibition titles include: "Dinos and Jake Chapman. GCSE Art Exam" at The Art Ginza Space, Tokyo, 2000; "Jackie and Denise Chapwoman. New Work", Modern Art, London, 2001; "The Rape of Creativity", Modern Art Oxford, 2003; "Explaining Christians to Dinosaurs", Kunsthaus Bregenz, 2005; and "Like a dog returns to its vomit", at White Cube, London, 2005. A major retrospective of their work has been organised by Tate Liverpool for 2006-07.

Jake and Dinos Chapman's work has been included in seminal group exhibitions such as "Sensation: Young British Artists from the Saatchi collection", London, Berlin and New York, 1997-99; as well as in "'Brilliant!' New Art from London", Minneapolis and Houston, 1995-96. It was in this exhibition that the public came to see their sculpture *Ubermensch* (1995). Here an effigy of the famous British physicist and mathematician Stephen Hawking in his wheelchair is balanced dangerously on a cliff-edge, like the stag standing on a rocky outpost in Edwin Landseer's *Monarch of the Glenn* (1851). Hawking is defamed, despite his 'super-human' intellect and elevation, his precarious positioning underpins his frail physicality. Regardless of the scientist's renowned models, such as the theory of "no boundary condition", or the idea that the universe is finite but has no boundary in imaginary time, we are reminded of his mortality.

Recently, their work has come to attention again in more tragic circumstances through the destruction of *Hell* in 2004, arguably their most monumental sculptural work to date, which had been exhibited at the Royal Academy of Art, London's "Apocalypse" exhibition in 2000. Nonetheless, rather than being disheartened, the Chapmans continue to turn events and occurrences on their heads, and continue to offer new bodies of work which draw life on the peculiar legacy of others.

Futher reading:

"Jake & Dinos Chapman. Works from the Chapman Family Collection". Essay by Suhail Malik. Jay Jopling / White Cube, London, 2002
"Jake & Dinos Chapman". Texts by Eckhard Schneider, Jake Chapman, James Hall and Rudolf Sagmeister. Kunsthaus Bregenz, 2005
"Jake and Dinos Chapman". Tate Publishing, London, 2006

杰克·查普曼和迪诺斯·查普曼 / Jake and Dinos Chapman

杰克·查普曼和迪诺斯·查普曼
查普曼家族收藏－素描III
2002
黑白版画
148.6cm×128.6cm
艺术家以及Jay Jopling／伦敦白色立方画廊借予展出
© 艺术家
照片：Gareth Winters

Jake and Dinos Chapman
Drawing III from the Chapman Family Collection
2002
Black and white etching
148.6cm×128.6cm
Courtesy the artist and Jay Jopling/White Cube, London
© the artists
Photo: Gareth Winters

杰克·查普曼和迪诺斯·查普曼 / Jake and Dinos Chapman

杰克·查普曼和迪诺斯·查普曼
查普曼家族收藏－素描IV
2002
黑白版画
148.6cm×128.6cm
艺术家以及Jay Jopling / 伦敦白色立方画廊借予展出
© 艺术家
照片：Gareth Winters

Jake and Dinos Chapman
Drawing IV from the Chapman Family Collection
2002
Black and white etching
148.6 cm×128.6 cm
Courtesy the artist and Jay Jopling/White Cube, London
© the artists
Photo: Gareth Winters

杰克·查普曼和迪诺斯·查普曼
查普曼家族收藏－素描IV

杰克·查普曼和迪诺斯·查普曼 / Jake and Dinos Chapman

杰克·查普曼和迪诺斯·查普曼
查普曼家族收藏—素描V
2002
黑白版画
148.6cm×128.6cm
艺术家以及Jay Jopling / 伦敦白色立方画廊借予展出
© 艺术家
照片：Gareth Winters

Jake and Dinos Chapman
Drawing V from the Chapman Family Collection
2002
Black and white etching
148.6cm×128.6 cm
Courtesy the artist and Jay Jopling/White Cube, London
© the artists
Photo: Gareth Winters

杰克·查普曼和迪诺斯·查普曼 / Jake and Dinos Chapman

杰克·查普曼和迪诺斯·查普曼
超级人物
1995
玻璃纤维、树脂和涂料
366cm×183cm×183cm
私人收藏，Jay Jopling / 伦敦白色立方画廊借予展出
© 艺术家

Jake and Dinos Chapman
Ubermensch
1995
Fibreglass, resin and paint
366cm×183cm×183cm
Private Collection courtesy Jay Jopling/White Cube, London
© the artists

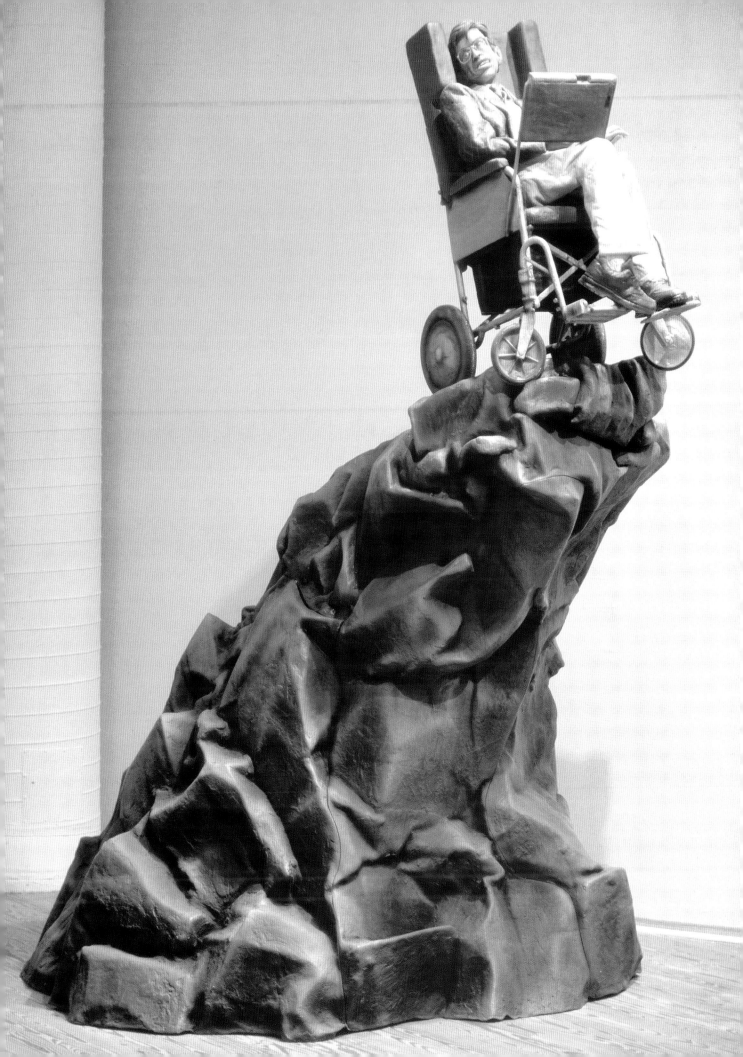

翠西・艾敏
Tracey Emin

翠西·艾敏
Jay Jopling / 伦敦白色立方画廊
摄影：Jake Gavin

Tracey Emin
Courtesy Jay Jopling/White Cube, London
Photo: Jake Gavin

翠西·艾敏 / Tracey Emin

翠西·艾敏1963年生于伦敦，在英国东南部海岸城市马尔盖特长大。1986-1989年，她在梅德史东艺术学院学习，1991年在伦敦皇家艺术学院获得硕士学位。艾敏1999年入围特纳奖候选人名单，并作为英国代表艺术家被选入2007年第52届威尼斯双年展。如今，艾敏在伦敦居住和创作。

翠西·艾敏是一位富有魄力并愿意和观众以更直接的方式进行沟通的艺术家。1994年，她和艺术家莎拉·卢卡斯一起在伦敦最东边开设了一家售卖艺术品的商店。1994年对艾敏来说也是独特和具有标志性的一年。她去美国旅行，途中对她的个人传记《对灵魂的探索》[Exploration of the Soul]，进行了阅读和录音。这件事被记录在一件名为《纪念碑山谷（大尺寸）》[Monument Valley (Grand Scale)] 的作品里（1995-1997年）。作品展示了在著名的亚利桑那沙漠山谷，艺术家坐在祖母的扶椅上阅读的画面。这把椅子被艾敏绣上了讲述她个人奇闻轶事的图像。作为一次自我发现和解析的旅程，艾敏在这次美国之行中，通过记述痛苦的个人经历治愈了自己的心灵创伤。后来，艾敏在这把椅子上绣上了她访问过的地点的名称，并将它作为一件参展艺术品，命名为《椅子能赚很多钱》[There's A Lot of Money in Chairs, 1994]。

翠西·艾敏的作品所使用的媒介极为广泛，包括绘画、录像、行为、摄影、版画复制、装置和刺绣等。她的作品包括自传文本，里边常有奇特的拼写错误、颠倒的词序，或是自相矛盾的语句。她的织物作品尤为典型：她选用一种与女性成就相关的媒介，将它倒置，以不典型的女性行为，对性别里对峙性的因素进行探讨。在《根本的事实》[The Simple Truth, 1995] 这个作品里，美国国旗下面绣着一行字"一直会在这儿"。这个作品也可以理解为对政治的批判，它使观众不得不提出一个问题：美国人在哪里"一直会在这儿"？确实，尽管美国试图全球多国移植它的文化，但艾敏在这儿想要表达的可能是一个美式泛滥的含义。

艾敏作品的煽动性，不在于它的形式，而在于它的主题。作品《我的床》[My Bed, 1998]，在创作后的第二年（1999年）成为她在英国泰特美术馆的特纳奖展览上最为瞩目的作品。简单说来，它由艺术家还没有整理的床铺以及周围散落着的她卧室里的私人物件组成。艾敏的作品是一种自传式的、自然的情感的流露。她的作品常常表达一种焦虑，这种焦虑可以是悲剧性的，也可以是幽默的，她把创作材料作为一种心理过滤器。

翠西·艾敏的主题常常是一些我们不得不面对的问题，比如爱情、性、死亡。她讲述个人的苦难经历，尤其是对年轻的女性们讲述诸如强暴、堕胎、酗酒、性恐吓和暴力等事件。近期，艾敏创作了一部影片，名为《顶点》[Top Spot, 2004]，灵感来源于她的真实生活经历。以她的家乡马尔盖特作为背景，电影关注的是当今英国年轻人忧虑的问题。艾敏不断将事实和虚构、自传、个人得失与悲喜、冥想和对抗等主题交织在她大量的大胆创新的作品里。

艾敏的作品常常是重大群展的重要组成部分。曾参加的展览有："精彩！来自伦敦的新艺术"，明尼阿波利斯和休斯敦，1995-1996年；"感觉：萨奇收藏的英国青年艺术家作品"，伦敦、柏林和纽约，1997-1999年。这些展览中非常重要的一件作品是艾敏的《所有和我睡过的人》[Everyone I Have Ever Slept With 1963-1995, 1995]，这件作品是一个帐篷，里边绣着所有曾经和她分享过一张床的人的名字。

精选个展有：Gesellschaft für Aktuelle Kunst，德国不来梅，1999年；市立博物馆，阿姆斯特丹，2002年；现代美术馆，慕尼黑，2002年；牛津当代艺术馆，2002年；Platform Garanti当代艺术中心，伊斯坦布尔，2004年。

参考阅读：
"Tracey Emin"，Neal Brown, Sarah Kent, 以及Matthew Collings编写，Jay Jopling/白色立方画廊，伦敦，1998年
"The Art of Tracey Emin"，Mandy Merck、Chris Townsend等编写，Thames&Hudson出版社，2002年
"Tracey Emin"，Jeanette Winterson和 Rudi Fuchs编写，Rudi Fuchs and Tracey Emin与Carl Freedman的对话，Rizzoli出版社，纽约，2006年

Tracey Emin was born in London in 1963 and grew up in Margate on the South East coast of England. She studied at Maidstone College of Art, 1986-1989 and then completed an MA at the Royal College of Art, London in 1991. Emin was shortlisted for the Turner Prize in 1999 and has been selected to represent Britain at the 52nd Venice Biennale of Art, 2007. Emin lives and works in London.

Tracey Emin formed part of a generation of enterprising artists who wanted to reach their audience directly. In 1994 she held a collaborative 'shop' selling artworks with fellow artist Sarah Lucas in the East End of London. It was also a significant year as she travelled across the USA recording readings from her autobiography, "Exploration of the Soul". This performance is recorded in a work entitled *Monument Valley (Grand Scale)* (1995-97), which shows the artist seated reading the book in her late grandmother's chair, in the eponymous Arizonan desert valley. Emin had embroidered the chair with significant personal anecdotes. As a journey of self-discovery and analysis, Emin performed a healing ritual through recounting painful personal memories as she travelled across the United States. The chair was then also subsequently sewn with the names of the places she visited, and is exhibited as an artwork entitled *There's A Lot of Money in Chairs* (1994).

Tracey Emin works in a range of different media, including drawing, film, performance, photography, printmaking, installation and appliqué. Her work includes autobiographical text, often with idiosyncratic spelling mistakes, word reversals, or paradoxical statements. Her textile works are particularly characteristic: she takes a medium associated with female accomplishment but turns it on its head to explore sexually explicit and confrontational issues uncharacteristic of model feminine behaviour. In *The Simple Truth* (1995), the statement "here to stay" is embroidered under the United States of America's flag. This work can also be read as a political critique - it begs the viewer to ask the question: where are the Americans "here to stay"? Indeed, here Emin is making a statement about American omnipresence perhaps though its global multinational implantation.

Emin's work is provocative, not so much in its form, but in its subject matter. *My Bed* (1998), which formed the central feature of her Turner Prize exhibition at Tate Britain the following year, consisted in short of the artist's unmade bed surrounded by personal items from her bedroom. Emin's work is disarmingly autobiographical and emotionally expressive. Often her work expresses angst, it can be tragic, yet it can also be humorous, as she uses her working materials as a psychological filter.

Tracey Emin deals with confrontational themes such as love, sex, death. She describes personal hardship particular to young women today such as rape, abortion, drunkenness, sexual intimidation and violence. Recently Emin has produced a film, entitled *Top Spot* (2004), which is loosely inspired by her real-life experiences. Set in her hometown Margate, the film discusses issues of concern to contemporary British teenagers. Emin continuously weaves fact and fiction, autobiography, personal loss and joy, meditation and confrontation in her bold body of work.

Emin's work featured in important group shows such as " 'Brilliant!' New Art from London", Minneapolis and Houston, 1995-96 and "Sensation: Young British Artists from the Saatchi collection", London, Berlin and New York, 1997-99. These exhibitions featured *Everyone I Have Ever Slept With 1963-1995* (1995), a tent appliquéd with the names of each person Emin had shared a bed with.

Major solo exhibitions include: Gesellschaft für Aktuelle Kunst, Bremen,1999; Stedelijk, Amsterdam, 2002; Haus der Kunst, München, 2002; Modern Art Oxford, 2002; Platform Garanti Contemporary Arts Center, Istanbul, 2004.

Further reading:
"Tracey Emin". Texts by Neal Brown, Sarah Kent and Matthew Collings. Jay Jopling/White Cube, London, 1998
"The Art of Tracey Emin". Edited by Mondy Merck, Chris Townsend et al. Thames & Hudson, 2002.
"Tracey Emin". Texts by Jeanette Winterson. Rudi Fuchs and Tracey Emin in conversation with Carl Freedman. Rizzoli, New York, 2006

翠西 · 艾敏 / Tracey Emin

翠西 · 艾敏
纪念碑山谷（大尺寸）
1995–1997
乙烯基铝上照片
122cm×183cm
泰特收藏，伦敦
© 艺术家
照片：艺术家和Jay Jopling / 伦敦白色立方画廊借予展出

Tracey Emin
Monument Valley (Grand Scale)
1995-97
Photograph on vinyl on aluminium
122cm×183cm
Tate Collection, London
© the artist
Photo: courtesy the artist and Jay Jopling/ White Cube, London

翠西 · 艾敏 / Tracey Emin

翠西 · 艾敏
椅子能赚很多钱
1994
绣花扶手椅
69cm×53.5cm×49.5cm
私人收藏，Jay Jopling / 伦敦白色立方画廊借予展出
© 艺术家

Tracey Emin
There's A Lot of Money in Chairs
1994
Appliquéd armchair
69cm×53.5cm×49.5cm
Private Collection courtesy Jay Jopling/White Cube, London
© the artist

翠西・艾敏 / Tracey Emin

翠西・艾敏
根本的事实
1995
羊毛，棉布料，毡布
216cm×235cm
艺术委员会收藏， Hayward画廊，伦敦
© 艺术家

Tracey Emin
The Simple Truth
1995
Wool, cotton, felt
216cm×235cm
Arts Council Collection, Hayward Gallery, London
© the artist

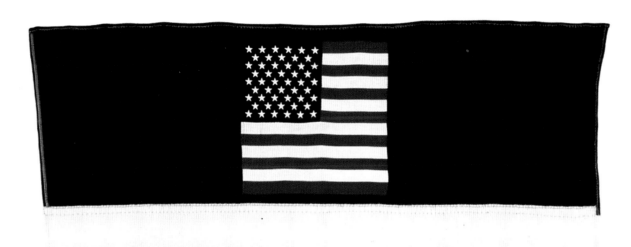

道格拉斯·戈登
Douglas Gordon

道格拉斯·戈登

道格拉斯·戈登
像柯特·科本、安迪·沃霍尔、米拉·亨德利、玛丽莲·梦露一样的自画像
1996
手绘彩色相片
75cm×75cm
艺术家本人和伦敦Lisson画廊

Douglas Gordon
Self Portrait as Kurt Cobain as Andy Warhol as Myra Hindley as Marilyn Monroe
1996
Colour hand photographic print
75cm×75 cm
Courtesy the artist and Lisson Gallery, London

道格拉斯·戈登 / Douglas Gordon

道格拉斯·戈登1966年出生在苏格兰格拉斯哥，1984年至1988年在格拉斯哥艺术学校学习，之后1988年到1990年就读于伦敦史莱德艺术学校。他于1996年获得特纳奖，1997年获得威尼斯双年展"Premio 2000"大奖。1997年至1998年他还参与了德国汉诺威和柏林的德国学术交流中心国际艺术家项目。戈登如今在纽约居住和创作。

戈登的作品探讨的是重大的主题，他尤其关注伦理两分的问题，比如宗教与信仰、善良与邪恶、无罪与犯罪、生命与死亡等。戈登经常用他的身体作为辩论的依据，探讨人性的自相矛盾，并使观众在他的调查过程中扮演神甫和证人的角色。他审视着意义交流的方式以及集体意识决定认知的方式。

戈登运用的是原版和再创作电影胶片以及其他媒介，包括电视、摄影、文本和雕塑。《24小时惊魂记》[24 Hour Psycho, 1993]也许是他早期最为著名的作品。在这个作品里，他把电影大师希区柯克的同名电影《惊魂记》放慢延长至24小时，由此延长了每一帧画面的戏剧张力，从而有效地改变了影片的含义。而且，由于原电影里的角色关系发生移位，致使观众重新来考虑来影片的含义。

在作品《10米／秒》[10 ms $^{-1}$, 1994]里，戈登借用了源于第一次世界大战的医学胶片元素。在片中，第一眼看去，一个男人似乎正在进行体操训练。随着情节的发展，他的身体不断地痉挛抽搐，每一次试图站立起来都以失败告终。到这时观众才开始意识到这个男人也许是一个外伤致残的受害者。通过放慢或者循环原版电影胶片来增加悬念，戈登想要论证的是，我们对环境的感知来源于它呈现在我们眼前的方式。对内容的抽离，改变了电影的含义，而观众则感觉像是一个偷窥某种可怜处境的旁观者。作品名称来源于一个物体在地心引力的作用下坠落的速度，比如身体正常落下的速度。

《收尸人》[Croque Mort, 2000] 则扩展了戈登用自身作为研究依据的兴趣，因为他在这个作品中拍摄了自己刚刚出生的女儿。重复也是戈登在作品中表现出的另一个兴趣，这个包括七张照片在内的系列作品表现的是一个具有强烈效果的自我封闭的视觉装置。事实上，这个作品被安置在一间完全是红色的房间里，就像一个铺满红地毯的电影院，或者说像一个子宫的内部。根据传说，"croque mort"，即法文里的收尸人，会在人们刚刚离世时咬他们的脚，以检验他们是否真的死了，因此得名为"咬死人的人"。在这个系列作品里，戈登的女儿咬着自己的脚和手指玩，虽然这只是一个新生儿出于天性在对自身的生理存在进行确认，但戈登通过对这种行为的高度特写以及赋予作品这个具有邪恶意味的标题，从而提醒我们生理机体的死亡必然性。因此，这个本来可以让人心生怜爱之情的婴儿系列照片，却让观众产生了意想不到的体验。

近期，戈登和另外一位艺术家菲利浦·帕雷诺共同制作了一部关于法国足球传奇人物齐内丹·齐达内的影片，名字叫做《齐达内，一幅21世纪的肖像》[Zidane, Un portrait du 21ème siècle, 2006]。这部影片的长度刚好相当于一场足球比赛的时间，影片集中锁定在齐达内一个人身上——随着比赛的进行，影片对齐达内的情绪和反应进行跟踪。这部影片进一步发展了艺术家对于艺术、电影和影院之间关系的兴趣。

近期精选的个展有：黑瓦德画廊，伦敦和苏格兰国立美术馆，爱丁堡，2000年；巴黎市立当代美术馆，1993年和2000年；利物浦泰特美术馆，2000年；米罗美术基金会，巴塞罗那，2006年；现代艺术博物馆，纽约，2006年。

参考阅读：
"Douglas Gordon"，Katrina M.Brown 编写，当代艺术家系列，泰特出版社，伦敦，2004年
"Douglas Gordon: Confessions by Douglas Gordon and James Hogg"，波坚思美术馆，2006年
"Douglas Gordon: Timeline"，Klaus Biesenbach 等人编写，纽约现代艺术博物馆，纽约，2006年

Douglas Gordon was born in Glasgow, Scotland in 1966. He studied at the Glasgow School of Art, 1984-88, and then at the Slade School of Art, London, 1988-90. He was awarded the Turner Prize in 1996, the Premio 2000 at the Venice Biennale, 1997. He also undertook a DAAD International Artists Programme in Hanover and Berlin, 1997-8. Gordon lives and works in New York.

Gordon's work explores major themes, in particular ethical dichotomies such as religion and faith, good and evil, innocence and guilt, life and death. Gordon often uses his body as a ground for debate, exploring how contradictory human nature can be, and involves the viewer in the manner of a confessor and witness to his investigations. He examines the way in which meaning is communicated and how perception is defined by collective consciousness.

Gordon works with original and found cinematic footage, as well as other media, including video, photography, text and sculpture. His most renowned early work is perhaps *24 hour Psycho* (1993). In this work he slowed down Alfred Hitchcock's eponymous film to last for the duration of 24 hours. This effectively changes the meaning of the film, as it lengthens the dramatic tension within each frame. It also makes the viewer reconsider the sense of the film as the relationship between the characters in the original film is shifted.

In *10 ms $^{-1}$* (1994), Gordon appropriated medical footage dating from the First World War. Here, a man seems at first glance to be undertaking gymnastic exercise. As the sequence progresses, his body continues to jerk and flail, and as he continually fails to manage to stand up, the viewer comes to realise that this person might be the victim of a traumatic injury. Increasing the suspense by slowing down and looping the original footage, Gordon demonstrates that our perception of a situation is inherent in the way it is presented to us. Taken out of context the meaning of the film is altered and the viewer is made to feel like a voyeur of a pathetic situation. The title is a reference to the speed at which an object falls under the pull of gravity, the speed at which a body for example would normally fall.

Croque Mort (2000) extends Gordon's interest in using his own body as a ground of investigation as, here, he has photographed his newly born daughter. Repetition is also an ongoing interest in Gordon's work, and this series of seven photographs provides a powerful self-contained visual installation. Indeed, the works are installed in a wholly red room, like a cinema room with its red carpet, or the inside of a womb. A 'croque mort', or undertaker in French, was the person who as legend has it, would bite the feet of the recently deceased to check whether they were effectively dead, hence the appellation 'the one who bites the dead'. In this series, Gordon's daughter playfully bites her own feet and fingers, but with the extreme close up and with the addition of the sinister title, what is simply a newborn's natural checking of its physical existence actually turns into a reminder of our physical mortality. What could be a sentimental series of images of a baby is turned into an unexpected experience.

Recently, Gordon has co-produced *Zidane, Un portrait du 21ème siècle* (2006), with artist Philippe Parreno, a film about the French footballing legend Zinedine Zidane. The film, which is the length of a football match, concentrates solely on the single figure of Zidane – it follows his moods and reactions as the game progresses, and is a further development of the artist's interest in the relation between fine art, film and cinema.

Recent selected solo exhibitions include: Hayward Gallery, London and National Galleries of Scotland, Edinburgh, 2000; Musée d'Art Moderne de la Ville de Paris, 1993 and 2000; Tate Liverpool, 2000; Fundació Joan Miró, Barcelona, 2006 and the Museum of Modern Art, New York, 2006.

Further reading:
"Douglas Gordon". Texts by Katrina M. Brown. Modern Artists series, Tate publishing, London, 2004
"Douglas Gordon: Confessions by Douglas Gordon and James Hogg". Kunsthaus Bregenz, 2006
"Douglas Gordon: Timeline". Texts by Klaus Biesenbach et al. Museum of Modern Art, New York, 2006

道格拉斯·戈登 / Douglas Gordon

道格拉斯·戈登
10米／秒
1994
录像装置
20分钟57秒
英国文化协会收藏
© 艺术家

Douglas Gordon
10 ms $^{-1}$
1994
Video Installation
Duration: 20 minutes 57 seconds
British Council Collection
© the artist

道格拉斯·戈登 / Douglas Gordon

道格拉斯·戈登
收刀人
2000
彩色冲印（×7）
每张91cm×134.5cm（纵向，横向）
艺术委员会收藏，Hayward画廊，伦敦
© 艺术家

Douglas Gordon
Croque Mort
2000
7 C-Type photographic prints
91cm×134.5cm (portrait or landscape)
Arts Council Collection, Hayward Gallery, London
© the artist

莫娜·哈透姆 / Mona Hatoum

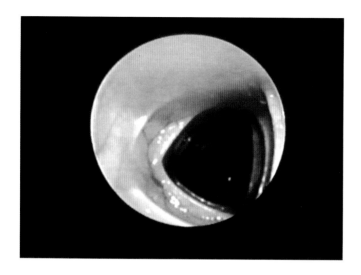

莫娜·哈透姆
陌生的身体
1994
录像装置，圆木结构，投影仪，录像放映机，音箱，四个扬声器
350cm×300cm×300cm
艺术家和Jay Jopling / 伦敦白色立方画廊借予展出
© 艺术家
照片：Philippe Migeat，巴黎蓬皮杜艺术中心借予展出

Mona Hatoum
Corps étranger
1994
Video installation with cylindrical wooden structure,
video projector, video player, amplifier and four speakers
350cm×300cm×300cm
Courtesy of the artist and Jay Jopling/ White Cube, London
© the artist
Photo: Philippe Migeat courtesy Centre Pompidou, Paris

莫娜·哈透姆 / Mona Hatoum

莫娜·哈透姆
隔离
1993
软钢，金属丝
127cm×49.5cm×95.5cm
私人收藏，Jay Jopling / 伦敦白色立方画廊借予展出
© 艺术家

Mona Hatoum
Incommunicado
1993
Mild steel and wire
127cm×49.5cm×95.5cm
Private Collection courtesy Jay Jopling/White Cube, London
© the artist

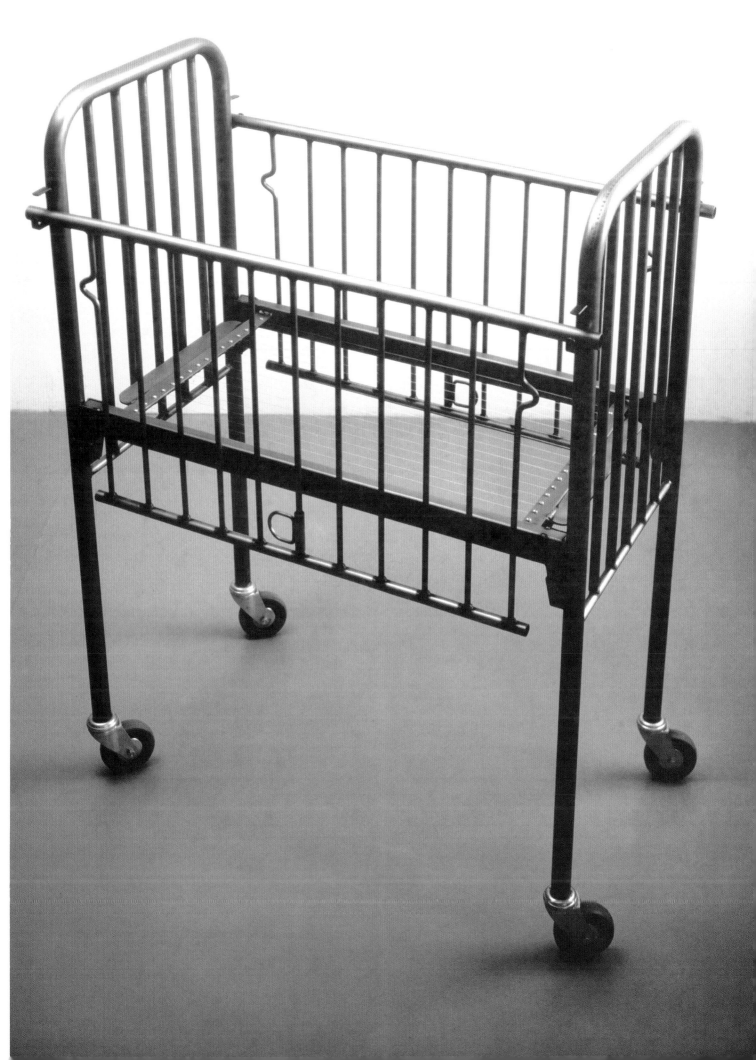

达明安·赫斯特 / Damien Hirst

达明安·赫斯特
对逃亡的后天无能
1992
玻璃，不锈钢，硅树脂，MDF桌子，椅子，烟灰缸，打火机以及香烟
213cm×305cm×205cm
伦敦Murderme借予展出
© 艺术家
照片：Prudence Cuming Associates股份有限公司

Damien Hirst
The Acquired Inability to Escape
1992
Glass, stainless steel, silicone, MDF table, chair, ashtray, lighter and cigarettes
213cm×305cm×205cm
Courtesy Murderme, London
© the artist
Photo: Prudence Cuming Associates

达明安·赫斯特
对逃亡的后天无能
玻璃，不锈钢，硅树脂，MDF桌子，椅子，烟灰缸，打火机以及香烟

加里·休姆 / Gary Hume

加里·休姆
户外的门画
1998
亮光漆，铝板
304.8cm×182.9cm (每个)
*Turnaround: Inside Out at the Hayward*展览现场照片，
Hayward画廊，伦敦，1998
© 艺术家
照片：Steve White

Gary Hume
Outside Door Paintings
1998
Gloss paint on aluminium panel
304.8cm×182.9cm (each)
Installation view, *Turnaround: Inside Out at the Hayward*,
Hayward Gallery, London, 1998
© the artist
photo: Steve White

加里·休姆 / Gary Hume

加里·休姆
户外的门画
1998
亮光漆，铝板
304.8cm×182.9cm
艺术家借予展出
© 艺术家
照片：Steve White

Gary Hume
Outside Door Painting
1998
Gloss paint on aluminium panel
304.8cm×182.9cm
Courtesy the artist
© the artist
Photo: Steve White

加里·休姆
户外的门画

亮光漆，铝板

莎拉·卢卡斯 / Sarah Lucas

莎拉·卢卡斯
吃香蕉
自画像印刷品系列
1990
水彩纸上的Iris印刷
60cm×80cm
英国文化协会收藏
© 艺术家

Sarah Lucas
Eating a Banana
From the Self-Portrait Print Portfolio
1990
Iris print on watercolour paper
60cm×80cm
British Council Collection
© the artist

莎拉·卢卡斯
神性
自画像印刷品系列
1991
水彩纸上的Iris印刷
60cm×80cm
英国文化协会收藏
© 艺术家

Sarah Lucas
Divine
From the Self-Portrait Print Portfolio
1991
Iris print on watercolour paper
60cm×80cm
British Council Collection
© the artist

莎拉·卢卡斯
自画像与·杯茶
自画像印刷品系列
1993
水彩纸上的Iris印刷
80cm×60cm
英国文化协会收藏
© 艺术家

Sarah Lucas
Self-Portrait with Mug of Tea
From the Self-Portrait Print Portfolio
1993
Iris print on watercolour paper
80cm×60cm
British Council Collection
© the artist

莎拉·卢卡斯
自画像与女内裤
自画像印刷品系列
1999
水彩纸上的Iris印刷
80cm×60cm
英国文化协会收藏
© 艺术家

Sarah Lucas
Self-Portrait with Knickers
From the Self-Portrait Print Portfolio
1999
Iris print on watercolour paper
80cm×60cm
British Council Collection
© the artist

莎拉·卢卡斯
自画像与煎鸡蛋
自画像印刷品系列
1996
水彩纸上的Iris印刷
80cm×60cm
英国文化协会收藏
© 艺术家

Sarah Lucas
Self-Portrait with Fried Eggs
From the Self-Portrait Print Portfolio
1996
Iris print on watercolour paper
80cm×60cm
British Council Collection
© the artist

莎拉·卢卡斯
人类厕所II
自画像印刷品系列
1996
水彩纸上的Iris印刷
80cm×60cm
英国文化协会收藏
© 艺术家

Sarah Lucas
Human Toilet II
From the Self-Portrait Print Portfolio
1996
Iris print on watercolour paper
80cm×60cm
British Council Collection
© the artist

莎拉·卢卡斯
以火灭火
自画像印刷品系列
1997
水彩纸上的Iris印刷
80cm×60cm
英国文化协会收藏
© 艺术家

Sarah Lucas
Fighting Fire with Fire
From the Self-Portrait Print Portfolio
1997
Iris print on watercolour paper
80cm×60cm
British Council Collection
© the artist

莎拉·卢卡斯
自画像与骷髅头
自画像印刷品系列
1996
水彩纸上的Iris印刷
80cm×60cm
英国文化协会收藏
© 艺术家

Sarah Lucas
Self-Portrait with Skull
From the Self-Portrait Print Portfolio
1996
Iris print on watercolour paper
80cm×60cm
British Council Collection
© the artist

莎拉·卢卡斯
有一条三文鱼#3
自画像印刷品系列
1997
水彩纸上的Iris印刷
80cm×60cm
英国文化协会收藏
© 艺术家

Sarah Lucas
Got a Salmon on #3
From the Self-Portrait Print Portfolio
1997
Iris print on watercolour paper
80cm×60cm
British Council Collection
© the artist

莎拉·卢卡斯
夏天
自画像印刷品系列
1998
水彩纸上的Iris印刷
80cm×60cm
英国文化协会收藏
© 艺术家

Sarah Lucas
Summer
From the Self-Portrait Print Portfolio
1998
Iris print on watercolour paper
80cm×60cm
British Council Collection
© the artist

莎拉·卢卡斯
抽烟
自画像印刷品系列
1998
水彩纸上的Iris印刷
80cm×60cm
英国文化协会收藏
© 艺术家

Sarah Lucas
Smoking
From the Self-Portrait Print Portfolio
1998
Iris print on watercolour paper
80cm×60cm
British Council Collection
© the artist

莎拉·卢卡斯
重访人类厕所
自画像印刷品系列
1998
水彩纸上的Iris印刷
80cm×60cm
英国文化协会收藏
© 艺术家

Sarah Lucas
Human Toilet Revisited
From the Self-Portrait Print Portfolio
1998
Iris print on watercolour paper
80cm×60cm
British Council Collection
© the artist

莎拉·卢卡斯 / Sarah Lucas

莎拉·卢卡斯
太空乳房
2000
丝网印刷壁纸
52cm×1000cm
英国文化协会收藏
© 艺术家

Sarah Lucas
Tits in Space
2000
Silk-screened wallpaper
52cm×1000cm
British Council Collection
© the artist

莎拉·卢卡斯
太空乳房
丝网印刷壁纸

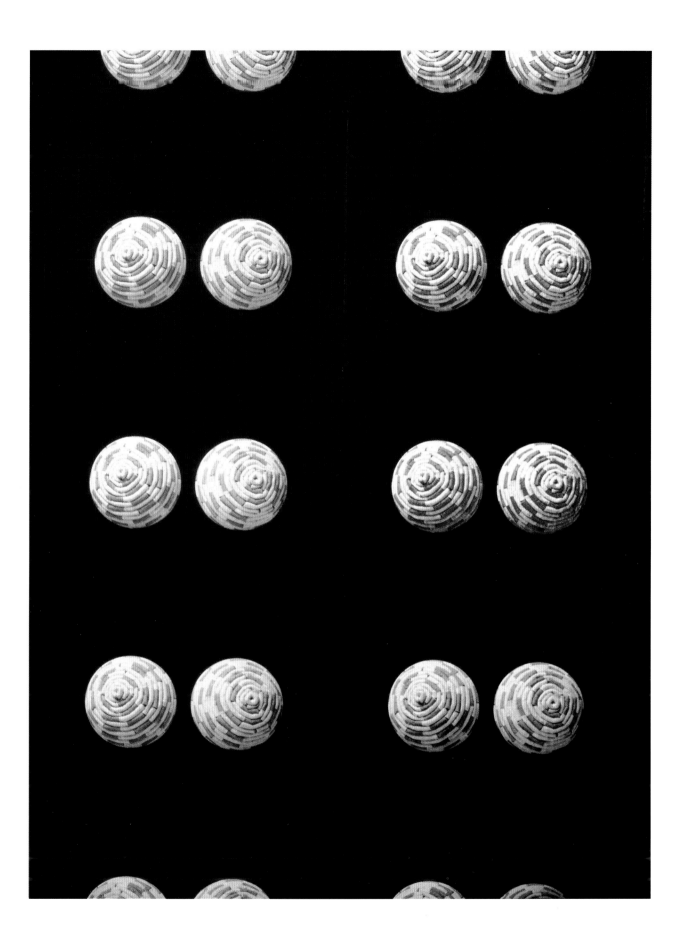

莎拉·卢卡斯 / Sarah Lucas

莎拉·卢卡斯
Donkey Kong Diddle Eye
2000
黑色沙发，荧光灯，壁灯
88cm×203cm×104cm
艺术家和Sadie Coles HQ画廊借予展出
© 艺术家

Sarah Lucas
Donkey-Kong-Diddle-Eye
2000
Black sofa, fluorescent lights, wall light
88cm×203cm×104cm
Courtesy the artist and Sadie Coles HQ, London
© the artist

马克·奎安 / Marc Quinn

马克·奎安
天真科学
2004
蜡，合成聚合物，干葡萄糖，分馏椰子油，混合红花油，菜子油，L-精氨酸，L-赖氨酸，L-天门冬氨酸盐，L-谷氨酸盐，乳化剂（E472（c）），L-白氨酸，柠檬酸三钾，磷酸二钙，L-苯丙氨酸，柠檬酸钠抗血凝剂，L-脯氨酸，L-缬氨酸,糖胶，L-异亮氨酸，N-乙酰-L-蛋氨酸，L-苏氨酸，氯化镁，L-组氨酸，L-丝氨酸，L-丙氨酸，氯化钾，L-色氨酸，酒石酸氢胆碱，L-酪氨酸，氯化钠，L-胱氨酸，牛磺酸，抗坏血酸维生素C，硫酸亚铁，L-肉碱，硫酸锌，肌糖，烟碱，DL-α-生育酚醋酸脂，D-泛钙酸，硫酸铜，硫酸锰，维生素B6，核黄素，维生素A醋酸脂，叶酸，碘化钾，亚硒酸钠，钼酸钠，维生素K1，生物素，氯化铬，维生素D3，维生素B12
25cm×68cm×32.5cm
Jay Jopling / 白色立方画廊借予展出
© 艺术家
照片：Stephen White

Marc Quinn
Innoscience
2004
Wax, Synthetic Polymer, Dried Glucose Syrup, Fractionated Coconut Oil, Hybrid Safflower Oil, Canola Oil, L-Arginine, L-Lysine, L-Aspartate, L-Glutamine, Emulsifier (E472 (c)), L-Leucine, Tripotassium Citrate, Calcium Phosphate Dibasic, L-Phenylalanine, Trisodium Citrate, L-Proline, L-Valine, Glycine, L-Isoleucine, N-Acetyl-L-Methionine, L-Threonine, Magnesium Chloride, L-Histidine, L-Serine, L-Alanine, Potassium Chloride, L-Tryptophan, Choline Bitartrate, L-Tyrosine, Sodium Chloride, L-Cystine, Taurine, Ascorbic Acid, Ferrous Sulphate, L-Carnitine, Zinc Sulphate, Inositol, Nicotinamide, DL-Alpha Tocopheryl Acetate, Calcium-D-Pantothenate, Copper Sulphate, Manganese Sulphate, Pyridoxine Hydrochloride, Riboflavin, Vitamin A Acetate, Folic Acid, Potassium Iodide, Sodium Selenite, Sodium Molybdate, Vitamin K1, Biotin, Chromium Chloride, Vitamin D3, Cyanocobalamin
25cm×68cm×32.5cm
Private Collection courtesy Jay Jopling/White Cube, London
© the artist
Photo: Stephen White

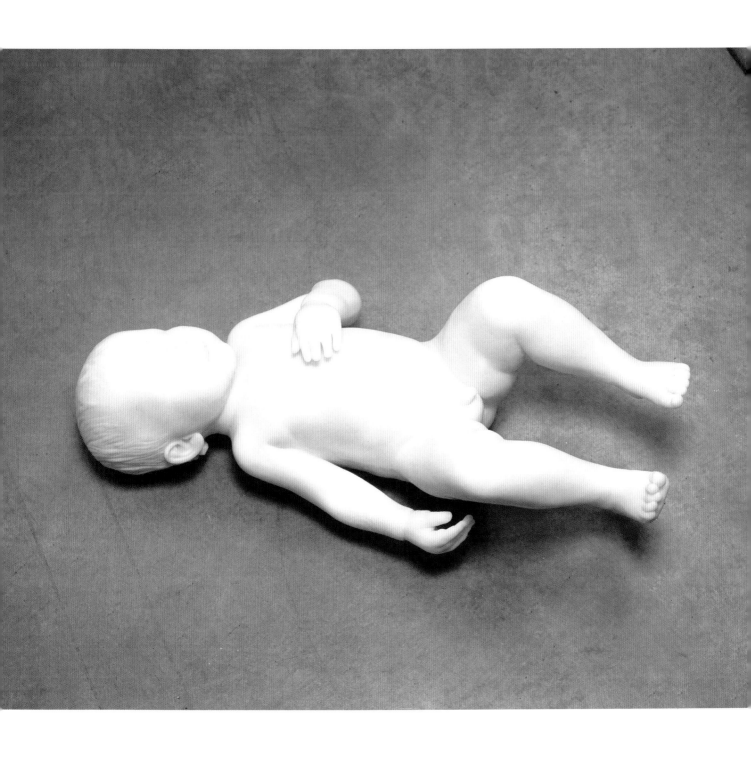

山姆·泰勒-伍德 / Sam Taylor-Wood

山姆·泰勒-伍德
升天
2003
35mm录像 / DVD机
4分钟15秒
Jay Jopling / 伦敦白色立方画廊借予展出
© 艺术家

Sam Taylor-Wood
Ascension
2003
35mm film/DVD projection
Duration: 4 minutes 15 seconds
Courtesy Jay Jopling/White Cube, London
© the artist

马克·渥林格 / Mark Wallinger

马克·渥林格
皇家爱斯科赛马会
1994
录像装置
录像显示器装置和航空箱各四个
3分钟41秒（循环）
英国文化协会收藏
© 艺术家

Mark Wallinger
Royal Ascot
1994
Video Installation
4 video monitors and 4 flight cases
Duration: 3 minutes 41 seconds (loop)
British Council Collection
© the artist

马克·渥林格
皇家爱斯科赛马会

录像装置
录像显示器装置和航空箱各四个

马克·渥林格 / Mark Wallinger

马克·渥林格
通向王国之门
2000
录像装置
11分钟10秒
艺术家和伦敦Anthony Reynolds画廊借予展出
© 艺术家

Mark Wallinger
Threshold to the Kingdom
2000
Video Installation
Duration: 11 minutes 10 seconds
Courtesy the artist and Anthony Reynolds Gallery, London
© the artist

吉莉安・韦英 / Gillian Wearing

吉莉安・韦英
60分钟的沉默
1996
录像，投影和声效系统
60分钟
艺术委员会收藏，Hayward画廊，伦敦
© 艺术家
照片：Maureen Paley画廊

Gillian Wearing
Sixty Minute Silence
1996
Video projection with sound
Duration: 60 minutes
Arts Council Collection, Hayward Gallery, London
© the artist
Photo: courtesy Maureen Paley, London

吉莉安・韦英
60分钟的沉默
录像，投影和声效系统

吉莉安・韦英 / Gillian Wearing

吉莉安・韦英
能说出你真实想法的标语，而不是让你言不由衷的标语
世界上的一切都是有联系的，关键是你要意识到它并且理解它
1992-1993
反转彩色冲印
152cm×103cm
英国文化协会收藏
© 艺术家
照片：伦敦Maureen Paley画廊借予展出

Gillian Wearing
Signs that Say What You Want Them To Say and Not Signs that Say What Someone Else Wants You To Say
EVERYTHING IS CONNECTED IN LIFE THE POINT IS YOU KNOW IT AND UNDERSTAND IT
1992-93
R-Type colour print
152cm×103cm
British Council Collection
© the artist
Photo: courtesy Maureen Paley, London

EVERYTHING
IS CONNECTED
IN LIFE
THE POINT IS TO
KNOW IT AND TO
UNERSTAND IT.

吉莉安·韦英 / Gillian Wearing

吉莉安·韦英
能说出你真实想法的标语，而不是让你言不由衷的标语
英国能够安然度过这个衰落时期吗？
1992-1993
反转彩色冲印
155cm×107cm
英国文化协会收藏
© 艺术家
照片：伦敦Maureen Paley画廊

Gillian Wearing
Signs that Say What You Want Them To Say and Not Signs that Say
What Someone Else Wants You To Say
WILL BRITAIN GET THROUGH THIS RECESSION?
1992-93
R-Type colour print
155cm×107cm
British Council Collection
© the artist
Photo: courtesy Maureen Paley, London

参展作品 /List of Works

参展作品 / List of Works

杰克・查普曼和迪诺斯・查普曼
查普曼家族收藏－素描III
2002
黑白版画
148.6cm×128.6cm
艺术家以及Jay Jopling / 伦敦白色立方画廊借予展出

Jake and Dinos Chapman
Drawing III from the Chapman Family Collection
2002
Black and white etching
148.6cm×128.6cm
Courtesy the artist and Jay Jopling/White Cube, London

杰克・查普曼和迪诺斯・查普曼
查普曼家族收藏－素描IV
2002
黑白版画
148.6cm×128.6cm
艺术家以及Jay Jopling / 伦敦白色立方画廊借予展出

Jake and Dinos Chapman
Drawing IV from the Chapman Family Collection
2002
Black and white etching
148.6 cm×128.6 cm
Courtesy the artist and Jay Jopling/White Cube, London

杰克・查普曼和迪诺斯・查普曼
查普曼家族收藏－素描V
2002
黑白版画
148.6cm×128.6cm
艺术家以及Jay Jopling / 伦敦白色立方画廊借予展出

Jake and Dinos Chapman
Drawing V from the Chapman Family Collection
2002
Black and white etching
148.6cm×128.6 cm
Courtesy the artist and Jay Jopling/White Cube, London

杰克・查普曼和迪诺斯・查普曼
超级人物
1995
玻璃纤维，树脂和涂料
366cm×183cm×183cm
私人收藏，Jay Jopling / 伦敦白色立方画廊借予展出

Jake and Dinos Chapman
Ubermensch
1995
Fibreglass, resin and paint
366cm×183cm×183cm
Private Collection courtesy Jay Jopling/White Cube, London

翠西・艾敏
椅子能赚很多钱
1994
绣花扶手椅
69cm×53.5cm×49.5cm
私人收藏，Jay Jopling / 伦敦白色立方画廊借予展出

Tracey Emin
There's A Lot of Money in Chairs
1994
Appliquéd armchair
69cm×53.5cm×49.5cm
Private Collection courtesy Jay Jopling/White Cube, London

翠西・艾敏
根本的事实
1995
羊毛，棉布料，毡布
216cm×235cm
艺术委员会收藏，Hayward画廊，伦敦

Tracey Emin
The Simple Truth
1995
Wool, cotton, felt
216cm×235cm
Arts Council Collection, Hayward Gallery, London

翠西·艾敏
纪念碑山谷（大尺寸）
1995－1997
乙烯基铝上照片
122cm×183cm
泰特收藏，伦敦

Tracey Emin
Monument Valley (Grand Scale)
1995-7
Photograph on vinyl on aluminium
122cm×183cm
Tate Collection, London

道格拉斯·戈登
10米／秒
1994
录像装置
20分钟57秒
英国文化协会收藏

Douglas Gordon
10 ms -1
1994
Video Installation
Duration: 20 minutes 57 seconds
British Council Collection

道格拉斯·戈登
收尸人
2000
彩色冲印（×7）
每张91cm×134.5cm（纵向，横向）
艺术委员会收藏，Hayward画廊，伦敦

Douglas Gordon
Croque Mort
2000
7 C-Type photographic prints
91cm×134.5cm (portrait or landscape)
Arts Council Collection, Hayward Gallery, London

莫娜·哈透姆
永不服输
1988－2002
聚氯乙烯底料喷绘
204.5cm×305cm
英国文化协会收藏

Mona Hatoum
Over My Dead Body
1988-2002
Ink Jet on PVC
204.5cm×305cm
British Council Collection

莫娜·哈透姆
隔离
1993
软钢，金属丝
127cm×49.5cm×95.5cm
私人收藏，Jay Jopling／伦敦白色立方画廊借予展出

Mona Hatoum
Incommunicado
1993
Mild steel and wire
127cm×49.5cm×95.5cm
Private Collection courtesy Jay Jopling/White Cube, London

达明安·赫斯特
女孩，喜欢男孩，喜欢女孩，喜欢女孩，就像女孩，喜欢男孩
2006
二联画：蝴蝶，手术刀片，剃须刀片，美工刀片，家用亮光漆，画布
直径：各213.36cm
艺术家和Jay Jopling／伦敦白色立方画廊借予展出

Damien Hirst
Girls, Who Like Boys, Who Like Boys, Who Like Girls, Like Girls, Like Boys
2006
Diptych: Butterflies, scalpel blades, razor blades, stanley blades and household gloss on canvas
Diameter: 213.36 cm (each)
Courtesy the artist and Jay Jopling/White Cube, London

参展作品 / List of Works

达明安・赫斯特
对逃亡的后天无能
1992
玻璃，不锈钢，硅树脂，MDF桌子，椅子，烟灰缸，打火机以及香烟
213cm×305cm×205cm
伦敦Murderme借予展出

Damien Hirst
The Acquired Inability to Escape
1992
Glass, stainless steel, silicone, MDF table, chair, ashtray, lighter and cigarettes
213cm×305cm×205cm
Courtesy Murderme, London

加里・休姆
户外的门画 I
1998
亮光漆，铝板
304.8cm×182.9cm
Turnaround: Inside Out at the Hayward展览现场照片，Hayward画廊，伦敦，1998
艺术家借予展出

Gary Hume
Outside Door Painting I
1998
Gloss paint on aluminium panel
304.8cm×182.9cm
Installation view, Turnaround: Inside Out at the Hayward, Hayward Gallery, London, 1998
Courtesy the artist

加里・休姆
户外的门画 II
1998
亮光漆，铝板
304.8cm×182.9cm
艺术家借予展出

Gary Hume
Outside Door Painting II
1998
Gloss paint on aluminium panel
304.8cm×182.9cm
Courtesy the artist

莎拉・卢卡斯
太空乳房
2000
丝网印刷壁纸
52cm×1000cm
英国文化协会收藏

Sarah Lucas
Tits in Space
2000
Silk-screened wallpaper
52cm×1000cm
British Council Collection

莎拉・卢卡斯
Donkey-Kong-Diddle-Eye
2000
黑色沙发，荧光灯，壁灯
88cm×203cm×104cm
艺术家和Sadie Coles HQ画廊借予展出

Sarah Lucas
Donkey-Kong-Diddle-Eye
2000
Black sofa, fluorescent lights, wall light
88cm×203cm×104cm
Courtesy the artist and Sadie Coles HQ, London

莎拉・卢卡斯
吃香蕉
自画像印刷品系列
1990
水彩纸上的Iris印刷
60cm×80cm
英国文化协会收藏

Sarah Lucas
Eating a Banana
From the Self-Portrait Print Portfolio
1990
Iris print on watercolour paper
60cm×80cm
British Council Collection

莎拉·卢卡斯
神性
自画像印刷品系列
1991
水彩纸上的Iris印刷
60cm×80cm
英国文化协会收藏

Sarah Lucas
Divine
From the Self-Portrait Print Portfolio
1991
Iris print on watercolour paper
60cm×80cm
British Council Collection

莎拉·卢卡斯
自画像与一杯茶
自画像印刷品系列
1993
水彩纸上的Iris印刷
80cm×60cm
英国文化协会收藏

Sarah Lucas
Self-Portrait with Mug of Tea
From the Self-Portrait Print Portfolio
1993
Iris print on watercolour paper
80cm×60cm
British Council Collection

莎拉·卢卡斯
自画像与女内裤
自画像印刷品系列
1999
水彩纸上的Iris印刷
80cm×60cm
英国文化协会收藏

Sarah Lucas
Self-Portrait with Knickers
From the Self-Portrait Print Portfolio
1999
Iris print on watercolour paper
80cm×60cm
British Council Collection

莎拉·卢卡斯
自画像与煎鸡蛋
自画像印刷品系列
1996
水彩纸上的Iris印刷
80cm×60cm
英国文化协会收藏

Sarah Lucas
Self-Portrait with Fried Eggs
From the Self-Portrait Print Portfolio
1996
Iris print on watercolour paper
80cm×60cm
British Council Collection

莎拉·卢卡斯
人类厕所II
自画像印刷品系列
1996
水彩纸上的Iris印刷
80cm×60cm
英国文化协会收藏

Sarah Lucas
Human Toilet II
From the Self-Portrait Print Portfolio
1996
Iris print on watercolour paper
80cm×60cm
British Council Collection

莎拉·卢卡斯
以火灭火
自画像印刷品系列
1997
水彩纸上的Iris印刷
80cm×60cm
英国文化协会收藏

Sarah Lucas
Fighting Fire with Fire
From the Self-Portrait Print Portfolio
1997
Iris print on watercolour paper
80cm×60cm
British Council Collection

参展作品 / List of Works

莎拉·卢卡斯
自画像与骷髅头
自画像印刷品系列
1996
水彩纸上的Iris印刷
80cm×60cm
英国文化协会收藏

Sarah Lucas
Self-Portrait with Skull
From the Self-Portrait Print Portfolio
1996
Iris print on watercolour paper
80cm×60cm
British Council Collection

莎拉·卢卡斯
有一条三文鱼#3
自画像印刷品系列
1997
水彩纸上的Iris印刷
80cm×60cm
英国文化协会收藏

Sarah Lucas
Got a Salmon on #3
From the Self-Portrait Print Portfolio
1997
Iris print on watercolour paper
80cm×60cm
British Council Collection

莎拉·卢卡斯
夏天
自画像印刷品系列
1998
水彩纸上的Iris印刷
80cm×60cm
英国文化协会收藏

Sarah Lucas
Summer
From the Self-Portrait Print Portfolio
1998
Iris print on watercolour paper
80cm×60cm
British Council Collection

莎拉·卢卡斯
抽烟
自画像印刷品系列
1998
水彩纸上的Iris印刷
80cm×60cm
英国文化协会收藏

Sarah Lucas
Smoking
From the Self-Portrait Print Portfolio
1998
Iris print on watercolour paper
80cm×60cm
British Council Collection

莎拉·卢卡斯
重访人类厕所
自画像印刷品系列
1998
水彩纸上的Iris印刷
80cm×60cm
英国文化协会收藏

Sarah Lucas
Human Toilet Revisited
From the Self-Portrait Print Portfolio
1998
Iris print on watercolour paper
80cm×60cm
British Council Collection

莎拉·卢卡斯
兔子
1997-2004
鞣革紧身衣，蓝色长筒袜，椅子，夹钳，丝绵，金属丝
96cm×64cm×72cm
私人收藏，Sadi Coles HQ画廊，伦敦

Sarah Lucas
Suffolk Bunny
1997-2004
Tan tights, blue stockings, chair, clamp, kapok, wire
96cm×64cm×72cm
Private Collection courtesy Sadie Coles HQ, London

马克·奎安
天真科学
2004
蜡，合成聚合物，干葡萄糖，分馏椰子油，混合红花油，菜子
油，L-精氨酸，L-赖氨酸，L-天门冬氨酸盐，L-谷氨酸盐，乳化剂
（E472（c）），L-白氨酸，柠檬酸三钾，磷酸二钙，L-苯丙氨酸，
柠檬酸钠抗血凝剂，L-脯氨酸，L-缬氨酸，糖胶，L-异亮氨酸，N-乙
酰-L-蛋氨酸，L-苏氨酸，氯化镁，L-组氨酸，L-丝氨酸，L-丙氨
酸，氯化钾，L-色氨酸，酒石酸氢胆碱，L-酪氨酸，氯化钠，L-胱
氨酸，牛磺酸，抗坏血酸维生素C，硫酸亚铁，L-肉碱，硫酸锌，
肌糖，烟碱，DL-α-生育酚醋酸脂，D-泛钙酸，硫酸铜，硫酸锰，
维生素B6，核黄素，维生素A醋酸脂，叶酸，碘化钾，亚硒酸钠，
钼酸钠，维生素K1，生物素，氯化铬，维生素D3，维生素B12
25cm×68cm×32.5cm
Jay Jopling / 白色立方画廊借予展出

Marc Quinn
Innoscience
2004
Wax, Synthetic Polymer, Dried Glucose Syrup, Fractionated Coconut
Oil, Hybrid Safflower Oil, Canola Oil, L-Arginine, L-Lysine, L-Aspartate,
L-Glutamine, Emulsifier (E472 (c)), L-Leucine, Tripotassium Citrate,
Calcium Phosphate Dibasic, L-Phenylalanine, Trisodium Citrate,
L-Proline, L-Valine, Glycine, L-Isoleucine, N-Acetyl-L-Methionine,
L-Theonine, Magnesium Chloride, L-Histidine, L-Serine, L-Alanine,
Potassium Chloride, L-Tryptophan, Choline Bitartrate, L-Tyrosine,
Sodium Chloride, L-Cystine, Taurine, Ascorbic Acid, Ferrous Sulphate,
L-Carnitine, Zinc Sulphate, Inositol, Nicotinamide, DL-Alpha Tocopheryl
Acetate, Calcium-D-Pantothenate, Copper Sulphate, Manganese
Sulphate, Pyridoxine Hydrochloride, Riboflavin, Vitamin A Acetate,
Folic Acid, Potassium Iodide, Sodium Selenite, Sodium Molybdate,
Vitamin K1, Biotin, Chromium Chloride, Vitamin D3, Cyanocobalamin
25cm×68cm×32.5cm
Private Collection courtesy Jay Jopling/White Cube, London

马克·奎安
红梅精神崩溃
1997
不锈钢，混凝土，聚亚氨酯，海绵
188cm×188cm×50.8cm
艺术家和Jay Jopling / 白色立方画廊借予展出

Marc Quinn
Raspberry Nervous Breakdown
1997
Stainless steel, concrete, polyurethane and sponges
188cm×188cm×50.8cm
Courtesy the artist and Jay Jopling/White Cube, London

山姆·泰勒–伍德
小小的死亡
2002
35mm录像 / DVD机
4分钟15秒
Jay Jopling / 伦敦白色立方画廊借予展出

Sam Taylor-Wood
A Little Death
2002
35mm film/DVD projection
Duration: 4 minutes 15 seconds
Courtesy Jay Jopling/White Cube, London

山姆·泰勒–伍德
升天
2003
35mm录像 / DVD机
4分钟15秒
Jay Jopling / 伦敦白色立方画廊借予展出

Sam Taylor-Wood
Ascension
2003
35mm film/DVD projection
Duration: 4 minutes 15 seconds
Courtesy Jay Jopling/White Cube, London

山姆·泰勒–伍德
轮回的五秒钟 VI
1996
彩色摄影，声效系统
72cm×757cm
英国文化协会收藏

Sam Taylor-Wood
Five Revolutionary Seconds VI
1996
Colour photograph on vinyl with sound
72cm×757cm
British Council Collection

参展作品 / List of Works

马克·渥林格
通向王国之门
2000
录像装置
11分钟10秒
艺术家和伦敦Anthony Reynolds画廊借予展出

Mark Wallinger
Threshold to the Kingdom
2000
Video Installation
Duration: 11 minutes 10 seconds
Courtesy the artist and Anthony Reynolds Gallery, London

马克·渥林格
皇家爱斯科赛马会
1994
录像装置
录像显示器装置和航空箱各四个
3分钟41秒（循环）
英国文化协会收藏

Mark Wallinger
Royal Ascot
1994
Video Installation
4 video monitors and 4 flight cases
Duration: 3 minutes 41 seconds (loop)
British Council Collection

吉莉安·韦英
60分钟的沉默
1996
录像，投影和声效系统
60分钟
艺术委员会收藏，Hayward画廊，伦敦

Gillian Wearing
Sixty Minute Silence
1996
Video projection with sound
Duration: 60 minutes
Arts Council Collection, Hayward Gallery, London

吉莉安·韦英
能说出你真实想法的标语，而不是让你言不由衷的标语
世界上的一切都是有联系的，关键是你要意识到它并且理解它
1992-1993
反转彩色冲印
152cm×103cm
英国文化协会收藏

Gillian Wearing
Signs that Say What You Want Them To Say and Not Signs that Say What Someone Else Wants You To Say
EVERYTHING IS CONNECTED IN LIFE THE POINT IS YOU KNOW IT AND UNDERSTAND IT
1992-93
R-Type colour print
152cm×103cm
British Council Collection

吉莉安·韦英
能说出你真实想法的标语，而不是让你言不由衷的标语
英国能够安然度过这个衰落时期吗？
1992-1993
反转彩色冲印
155cm×107cm
英国文化协会收藏

Gillian Wearing
Signs that Say What You Want Them To Say and Not Signs that Say What Someone Else Wants You To Say
WILL BRITAIN GET THROUGH THIS RECESSION?
1992-93
R-Type colour print
155cm×107cm
British Council Collection

图书在版编目（CIP）数据

余震：英国当代艺术展 1990-2006/英国大使馆文化教育处编. —长沙：湖南美术出版社，2007.3
ISBN 978-7-5356-2583-0

I. 余… II. 英… III. 艺术—作品综合集—英国—现代   IV. J156.11
中国版本图书馆CIP数据核字（2007）第020434号

余震: 英国当代艺术展 1990-2006
编者：英国大使馆文化教育处
责任编辑：吴海恩
责任校对：徐盾
出版发行：湖南美术出版社
地址：湖南省长沙市东二环一段622号
经销：湖南省新华书店
印刷：北京汇昌联创彩印有限公司
开本：889×1194 1/16
印张：10
版次：2007年3月第1版 2007年3月第1次印刷
印数：1-2500册
书号：ISBN 978 - 7 - 5356 -2583-0
——————————————

定价：80.00 元

www.britishcouncil.org.cn

定价：80.00 元

ISBN 978-7-535

9 787535 625830 >